500 YEARS OF INDIGENOUS RESISTANCE

GORD HILL

500 YEARS OF INDIGENOUS RESISTANCE

Cover and interior design by Daniel Meltzer

10 9 8 7 6 5 4 3

Library of Congress Control Number: 2009901389

ISBN 978-1-60486-106-8

Published by:
PM Press
PO Box 23912
Oakland, CA 94623
www.pmpress.org

Printed in the USA

TABLE OF CONTENTS

FOREWORD

Sixteen years after it was originally published in the first issue of the revolutionary Indigenous newspaper OH-TOH-KIN, *500 Years of Indigenous Resistance* remains an important and relevent history of the colonization of the Americas and the resistance to it. It begins with the arrival of Columbus and finishes with the resistance struggles that defined the early nineties; the Lubicons, the Mohawks, and the Campaign For 500 Years Of Resistance that occurred all over the Americas, and was a historical precurser to the well-known Zapatista uprising of 1994.

This pamphlet also includes artwork by the author, native artist, activist and former OH-TOH-KIN member Gord Hill.

500 YEARS OF INDIGENOUS RESISTANCE

This article is intended as a basic history of the colonization of the Americas since 1492, and the Indigenous resistance to this colonization continuing into 1992. The author admits to not having a full understanding of the traditions of his own people, the Kwakiutl (Kwakwaka'wakw); as such the article lacks an analysis based in an authentic Indigenous philosophy and is instead more of a historical chronology.

INTRODUCTION

Throughout the year 1992, the various states which have profited from the colonization of the Americas will be conducting lavish celebrations of the "Discovery of the Americas". Spain has spent billion of dollars for celebrations in conjunction with Expo '92 in Seville. In Columbus, Ohio, a $100 million quincentennial celebration plans on entertaining several million tourists. CELAM, the association of South America's Catholic bishops, has organized a gathering to celebrate the "fifth centenary of the evangelization of the Americas" to be presided over by the Pope. As well, there is a wide selection of museum exhibits, films, TV shows, books and many other products and activities focusing on Columbus and the "Discovery", all presenting one interpretation of the 500 years following 1492. The main thrust of this interpretation is that the colonization process—a process of genocide—has, with a few "bad spots", been overall a mutually beneficial process. The "greatness" of European religions and cultures was brought to the Indigenous peoples, who in return shared the lands and after "accidentally" being introduced to European disease, simply died off and whose descendants now fill the urban ghettos as alcoholics and welfare recipients. Of course, a few "remnants" of Indian cultures were retained, and there are even a few "professional" Indian politicians running around.

That was no "Discovery"—it was an American Indian Holocaust!

Until recently, commonly accepted population levels of the Indigenous peoples on the eve of 1492 were around 10–15 million. This number continues to be accepted by individuals and groups who see 1492 as a "discovery" in which only a few million Indians died—and then mostly from diseases. More recent demographic studies place the Indigenous population at between 70 to 100 million peoples, with some 10 million in North America, 30 million in Mesoamerica, and around 50 to 70 million in South America.

Today, in spite of 500 years of a genocidal colonization, there are an estimated 40 million Indigenous peoples in the Americas. In Guatemala, the Mayan peoples make up 60.3 percent of the population, and in Bolivia Indians comprise over 70 percent of the total population. Despite this, these Indigenous peoples lack any control over their own lands and comprise the most exploited and oppressed layers of the population, characteristics that are found also in other Indigenous populations in the settler states of the Americas (and throughout the world).

THE PRE-COLUMBIAN WORLD

Before the European colonization of the Americas, in that time of life scholars refer to as "Pre-history" or "Pre-Columbian", the Western hemisphere was a densely populated land. A land with its own peoples and ways of life, as varied and diverse as any of the other lands in the world. In fact, it was not even called "America" by those peoples. If there was any reference to the land as a whole it was as Turtle Island, or Cuscatlan, or Abya-Yala.

The First Peoples inhabited every region of the Americas, living within the diversity of the land and developing cultural lifeways dependent on the land. Their numbers approached 70–100 million peoples prior to the European colonization.[1]

Generally, the hundreds of different nations can be summarized within the various geographical regions they lived in. The commonality of cultures within these regions is in fact a natural development of people building lifeways dependent on the land. As well, there was extensive interaction and interrelation between the people in these regions, and they all knew each other as nations.

In the Arctic region live(d) the Inuit and Aleut, whose lifeways revolve(d) around the hunting of sea mammals (Beluga whales, walruses, etc.) and caribou, supplemented by fishing and trading with the people to the south.

South of the Arctic, in the Subarctic region of what is today Alaska, the Northwest Territories, and the northern regions of the Canadian provinces, live(d) predominantly hunting and fishing peoples. The varia-

---

1. Sources for the population of Indigenous peoples prior to 1492 include:
    - Henry F. Dobyns, *Native American Historical Demography: A Critical Bibliography*, University of Indiana Press, 1976; "Estimating Aboriginal Population: An Appraisal of Techniques with a New Hemispheric Estimate", *Current Anthropology*, No. 7, 1966.
    - Pierre Chanu, *Conquête et Exploitation de Nouveaux Mondes* (XVIe Siecle), Paris, 1969 (estimates population at 80–100 million).
    - William R. Jacobs, "The Tip of an Iceberg; Revisionism", in *William and Mary Quarterly*, No. 31, 1974 (estimates population at 50–100 million).
    - Woodrow Wilson Borah, "America as Model: The Demographic Impact of European Expansion Upon the Non-European World", in *Actas y Memorias XXXV Congreso Internacional de Americanistas*, Mexico, 1962 (estimates population at 100 million). Source: Roxanne Dunbar Ortiz, *Indians of the Americas*, Praeger Publishers, New York, 1984.

tions of these lands range from open tundra to forests and lakes, rivers, and streams. The Cree, Chipewyan, Kaska, Chilcotin, Ingalik, Beothuk, and many other nations inhabit(ed) this region, hunting bear, goats, and deer in the west, musk oxen and caribou further north, or buffalo further south in the prairies.

Altogether in the Arctic and Subarctic regions there lived perhaps as many as 100,000 people.

On the Pacific Northwest coast, stretching from the coasts of Alaska and British Columbia (BC) down to northern California, live(d) the Tlingit, Haida, Tsimshian, Kwakwaka'wakw, Nuu-chah-nulth, Nuxalk, Salish, Yurok, and many others. These peoples developed a lifeway revolving around fishing. The peoples of this region numbered as many as four million.

Between the Pacific coastal mountain range and the central plains in what is today southern BC, Washington, Oregon, Idaho and Montana, live(d) the Sahaptin (Nez Perce), Chopunnish, Shoshone, Siksikas (Blackfeet), and others. These peoples numbered around 200,000.

To the east were people of the plains, encompassing a vast region from Texas up to parts of southern Alberta, Saskatchewan, and Manitoba, eastward to North and South Dakota, Minnesota, Wisconsin, Missouri, and Arkansas. Here, the Lakota (Sioux), Cheyenne, Arapaho, plains Cree, Siksikas (of the Blackfeet Confederacy, including the Blood and Peigan), Crow, Kiowa, Shoshone, Mandan, and many others, numbered up to one million, and the buffalo as many as 80 million before their slaughter by the Europeans.

Further east, in the lands stretching from the Great Lakes to the Atlantic coast, live(d) hunting, fishing, and farming peoples; the Kanienkehake (Mohawks), Oneida, Onondaga, Cayuga, Seneca (these five nations formed the Haudenosaunee—the People of the Longhouse—also known as the Iroquois Confederacy), Ojibway, Algonkin, Micmac, Wendat (Huron), Potowatomi, Tuscarora, and others. In this woodland region, stretching from Ontario, Quebec, and New York, down to the Carolinas, lived up to two million peoples.

South of this area, from parts of the Virginias down to Florida, west of the Gulf of Mexico including Mississippi and Louisiana, live(d) the Muskogee-speaking Choctaw, Creek, and Chikasaw, the Cherokee, Natchez, Tonkawa, Atakapa, and others. One of the most fertile agricultural belts in the world, farming was well established supplemented by hunting and fishing. These peoples numbered between two and three million.

East of this area, in the southwestern United States, extending down to northern Mexico and California, live(d) agrarian and nomadic peoples: the Pueblo, Hopi, Zuni, the Yumun-speaking Hualapai, Mojave, Yuma, and Cocopa, the Uto-Aztecan speaking Pimas and Papagos, and the Athapascans consisting of the Navajo (Dine) and Apache peoples. These peoples, altogether, numbered about two million.

In the Mesoamerican region, including Mexico, Guatemala and Belize, live(d) the numerous agricultural peoples, whose primary staple was maize: the Aztecs, Texacoco, Tlacopan, and the Mayans—in the Yucatan peninsula. Here, large city-states with stone and brick buildings and pyramids, as well as extensive agrarian waterways consisting of dams and canals were built. Written languages were published in books, and the study of astronomy and mathematics was well established. A calendar system more accurate than any in Europe during the 15th century was developed. Altogether, these peoples numbered around 30–40 million.

In the Caribbean basin, including the coastal areas of Colombia, Venezuela, Costa Rica, Honduras, and the many small islands such as Cuba, Hispaniola, Puerto Rico etc., live(d) hunting, fishing, and agrarian peoples such as the Carib, Arawak, Warao, Yukpa, Paujanos, and others. These peoples numbered around five million.

In all of South America there were as many as 40–50 million peoples.

In the Andean highlands of Peru and Chile live(d) the Inca peoples, comprised of the Quechua and Aymara. In the south of Chile live(d) the Mapuche, and in the lowland regions—including the Amazon region—live(d) the Yanomami, Gavioe, Txukahame, Kreen, Akarore, and others. South of the Amazon region, in Argentina, Paraguay, and Uruguay, live(d) the Ayoreo, Ache, Mataco, Guarani, and many others. In the southernmost lands live(d) the Qawasgar, Selk'nam, Onu, and others.

With a few exceptions, the First Nations were classless and communitarian societies, with strong matrilineal features. The political sphere of Indigenous life was not dominated by men, but was in many cases the responsibility of women. Elders held a position of importance and honour for their knowledge. There were no prisons, for the First Nations peoples had well developed methods of resolving community problems, and there was—from the accounts of elders—very little in anti-social crime. Community decisions were most frequently made by consensus and discussions amongst the people.

But the First Nations were not perfect, being humans they had, and still have, their inconsistencies and practises that are not positive.

Some examples can be seen as the armed conflicts between nations throughout the Americas, and practises of slavery amongst the Pacific Northwest coast peoples and in the Mesoamerican region. However, even here the forms of warfare reflected similar developments throughout the world, and in any case never approached the genocidal methods developed, in particular, in Europe. Warfare was the practise of explicitly warrior societies. The accounts of slavery, although there is no way to explain it away, differed sharply from the Europeans in that it was not based on racism, nor was it a fundamental characteristic which formed the economic basis of these societies.

The history of the First Nations must always be analyzed critically; those who tell us that history are rarely ever of the Indigenous peoples.

THE GENOCIDE BEGINS

On October 12, 1492, sailing aboard the Santa Maria under finance from the Spanish crown, Cristoforo Colombo stumbled upon the island of Guanahani (believed to be San Salvador), in the Caribbean region. Initially charting a new trade route to Asian markets, the outcome of Colombo's voyage would quickly prove far more lucrative than the opening of new trade routes, as far as Europe was concerned.

It was on Guanahani that Colombo first encountered Taino Arawaks, whom he titled 'Indians', believing he had in fact reached Asia. For this initial encounter, Colombo's own log stands as testimony to his own greed:

> *"Their bodies swelled with greed, and their hunger was ravenous."*
> –Aztec testimonial

> No sooner had we concluded the formalities of taking possession of the island than people began to come to the beach... They are friendly and well-dispositioned people who bear no arms except for small spears.
>
> They ought to make good and skilled servants... I think they can easily be made Christians, for they seem to have no religion. If it pleases Our Lord, I will take six of them to Your Highnesses when I depart. (from Colombo's log, October 12, 1492)

True to his word, if little else, Colombo kidnapped about 9 Taino during his journey through the Bahamas, and anticipated even more kidnappings and enslavement,

> ...these people are very unskilled in arms. Your Highnesses will see this for yourselves when I bring you the seven that I have taken. After they learn our languages I shall return them, unless Your Highnesses order that the entire population be taken to Castille, or held captive here. With 50 men you could subject everyone and make them do what you wished.
> (Colombo's log, October 14, 1492) [3]

2. Robert H. Fuson, *The Log of Christopher Colombus*, International Marine Publishing Co., Maine, 1987, pg. 76.
3. Ibid, pg. 80. Colombo was inconsistent on the actual number of Taino he kidnapped.

Throughout Colombo's log of this first voyage, there is constant reference to the notion that the Taino believe the Europeans to be descended from heaven, despite the fact that [neither] Colombo nor any of his crew understood Arawak. Another consistency in Colombo's log is the obsession with gold, to which there are 16 references in the first two weeks alone, 13 in the following month, and 46 more in the next five weeks, despite the fact that Colombo found very little gold on either Guanahani or any of the other islands he landed on.

In a final reference to Colombo's log, one can also find the dual mission Colombo undertook:

> ...Your Highnesses must resolve to make them [the Taino—Oh-Toh-Kin ed.] Christians. I believe that if this effort commences, in a short time a multitude of peoples will be converted to our Holy Faith, and Spain will acquire great domains and riches and all of their villages. Beyond doubt there is a very great amount of gold in this country... Also, there are precious stones and pearls, and an infinite quantity of spices. (Colombo's log, November 11, 1492) [4]

The duality of Colombo's mission, and the subsequent European invasion that followed, was the Christianization of non-Europeans and the expropriation of their lands. The two goals are not unconnected; "Christianization" was not merely a program for European religious indoctrination, it was an attack on non-European culture (one barrier to colonization) and a legally and morally sanctioned form of war for conquest. "Even his name was prophetic to the world he encountered—Christopher Columbus translates to 'Christ-bearer Colonizer.'" [5]

Still on his first voyage, Colombo meandered around the Caribbean and eventually established the first Spanish settlement, 'Natividad', on the island of Hispaniola (today Haiti and the Dominican Republic). Leaving about 35 men on Hispaniola, Colombo and his crew returned to Spain to gather the materials and men needed for the coming colonization, and to report to the crown on his journey.

In September, 1493, Colombo returned to Hispaniola with a fleet of 17 ships and 1,200 men. The detachment that had been left on Hispaniola had been destroyed following outrages by the Spaniards against the Taino. The resistance had already begun.

---

4.   Ibid, pg. 107.
5.   *Akwesasne Notes*, Vol. 9, No. 4, 1977

Colombo would make four voyages in all, the remaining two in 1498 and 1502. His voyages around the Caribbean brought him to what is now Trinidad, Panama, Jamaica, Venezuela, Dominica, and several other islands—capturing Native peoples for slavery and extorting gold through a quota of a hawk's bell of gold dust to be supplied by every Native over the age of 14 every 3 months. Failure to fill the quota often entailed cutting the 'violators' hands off and leaving them to bleed to death. Hundreds of Carib and Arawak were shipped to Spain as slaves under Colombo's governorship, 500 alone following his second voyage. Indeed, the absence of a "great amount of gold" in the Caribbean had Colombo devising another method of financing the colonization: "The savage and cannibalistic Carib should be exchanged as slaves against livestock to be provided by merchants in Spain." (Letter to Queen Isabella)

Colombo died in 1506, but following his initial voyage to the Americas, wave upon wave of first Spanish, then Portuguese, Dutch, French and British expeditions followed, carrying with them conquistadors, mercenaries, merchants, and Christian missionaries.

Hispaniola served as the first beachhead, used by the Spanish as a staging ground for armed incursions and reconnaissance missions, justified through the 'Christianization' program; one year after Colombo's first voyage, Pope Alexander VI in his *Inter Cetera Divina Papal Bull* granted Spain all the world not already possessed by Christian states, excepting the region of Brazil, which went to Portugal.

While the Spanish laid the groundwork for their colonization plans, other European nations began to send their own expeditions.

In 1497, Giovanni Caboto Motecataluna (John Cabot), financed by England, crossed the Atlantic and charted the Atlantic coast of North America. Under the commission of Henry VII to "conquer, occupy, and possess" the lands of "heathens and infidels", Cabot reconnoitered the Newfoundland coast—kidnapping three Micmacs in the process.

At around the same time, Gaspar Corte Real, financed by Portugal, reconnoitered the Labrador and Newfoundland coasts, kidnapping 57 Beothuks to be sold as slaves to offset the cost of the expedition.

Meanwhile, Amerigo Vespucci—for whom the Americas were named—and Alonso de Ojedo, on separate missions for Spain, reconnoitered the West Indies and the Pacific coast of South America. Ojedo was actively carrying out slave raids, and was killed by a warrior's poisoned arrow for his efforts.

From the papal bull of 1493 and a subsequent Treaty of Tordesillas (1494), Portugal had been given possession of Brazil. In 1500, the Portuguese admiral Pedro Alvares Cabral formally claimed the land for the Portuguese crown.

Now that the initial reconnaissance missions had been completed, the invasion intensified and expanded. In 1513, Ponce de Leon, financed by Spain, attempted to land in Florida, but was driven off by 80 Calusa war canoes.

From 1517 to 1521, the Spanish conquistador Hernando Cortes laid waste to the Aztec empire in Mexico, capturing the capital city of Tenochtitlan and killing millions in a ruthless campaign for gold.

Shortly afterwards, in 1524, Pedro de Alvarado invaded the region of El Salvador, attacking the Cuscatlan, Pipeles, and Quiche peoples. In Guatemala Alvarado conducted eight major campaigns against the Mayans, and while he and his men were burning people alive, the Catholic priests accompanying him were busy destroying Mayan historical records (that is, while they weren't busy directing massacres themselves). Alvarado's soldiers were rewarded by being allowed to enslave the survivors.

In 1531, the Spaniard Francisco Pizarro invaded the region of the Incas (now Peru). Taking advantage of an internal struggle between two Inca factions led by the brothers Huascar and Atahualpa, Pizarro succeeded in subjugating the Incas by 1533.

Ten years later, Pedro de Valdivia claimed Chile for the Spanish crown, although fierce resistance by the Mapuche nation restricted the Spanish to the northern and central regions. Valdivia was eventually killed in battle by Mapuche warriors.

During this same period, Jacques Cartier, financed by France in 1534, was reconnoitering the eastern regions of what would become Canada, and Spaniards such as Hernando de Sotos, Marcos de Niza and others began penetrating into North America, claiming the lands for their respective countries, as was their custom.

EXPANSION, EXPLOITATION, AND EXTERMINATION

The formulative years of the colonization process were directed towards exploiting the lands and peoples to the fullest. To the Europeans, the Americas were a vast, unspoiled area suitable for economic expansion and exploitation.

The primary activity was the accumulation of gold and silver, then a form of currency among the European nations. This accumulation was first accomplished through the crudest forms of theft and plunder (i.e. Colombo's and Cortes' methods). Eventually, more systematic forms were developed, including the encomiendas—a form of taxation imposed on Indigenous communities that had been subjugated—and the use of Indigenous slaves to pan the rivers and streams. By the mid-1500s, the expropriation of gold and silver involved intensive mining. Entire cities and towns developed around the mines. Millions of Indigenous peoples died working as slaves in the mines at Guanajuato and Zacatecas in Mexico, and Potosi in Bolivia. By the end of the 1500s, Potosi was one of the largest cities in the world at 350,000 inhabitants. Peru was also another area of intensive mining. From the time of the arrival of the first European colonizers until 1650, 180–200 tons of gold—from the Americas—was added to the European treasury. In today's terms, that gold would be worth $2.8 billion.[6] During the same period, eight million slaves died in the Potosi mines alone.

"I am Smallpox... I come from far away...where the great water is and then far beyond it. I am a friend of the Big Knives who have brought me; they are my people."

–Jamake Highwater, *Anpao: an Indian Odyssey*

---

6.   Jack Weatherford, *Indian Givers*, Ballantine Books, New York, 1988.

Slavery was another major economic activity. Not only for work in the mines, but also for export to Europe. In Nicaragua alone, the first ten years of intensive slaving, beginning in 1525, saw an estimated 450,000 Miskitu and Sumu peoples shipped to Europe. Tens of thousands perished in the ships that transported them. Subsequently, the slave trade would turn to Afrika, beginning in the mid-1500s when Portuguese colonists brought Afrikan slaves to Brazil to cut cane and clear forest area for the construction of settlements and churches. An estimated 15 million Afrikan peoples would be brought as slaves to the Americas by 1800, and a further 40 million or so perished in the transatlantic crossing in the miserable conditions of the ships holds.

In areas such as the highlands of northern Chile, Peru, Guatemala, and Mexico, where the climate was more suitable, the Spanish were able to grow crops such as wheat, cauliflower, cabbage, lettuce, radish, sugar cane, and later grapes, bananas, and coffee. By the mid-1500s, using slave labour, many of these crops—particularly wheat and sugar cane—were large-scale exports for the European markets.

In other areas, sprawling herds of cattle were established. Herds which rarely exceeded 800 or 1,000 in Spain reached as many as 8,000 in Mexico. By 1579, some ranches in northern Mexico had up to 150,000 head of cattle.[7] The effects of extensive land-clearing for the crops and ranches and intensive mining culminated in increasing deforestation and damage to the lands. More immediately for the Indigenous peoples in the region, particularly those who lived on subsistence agriculture, was the dismantling of destruction of agrarian ways replaced by export crops.

In order to carry out this expansion and exploitation, the subjugation of the First Nations was a necessity, and the task of colonizing other peoples was one in which the Europeans had had plenty of experience.

> In a sense, the first people colonized under the profit motivation by the use of labour...were the European and English peasantry. Ireland, Bohemia and Catalonia were colonized. The Moorish nation, as well as the Judaic Sephardic nation, were physically deported by the Crown of Castille from the Iberian peninsula... All the methods for relocation, deportation and expropriation, were already practised if not perfected.[8]

Prior to Colombo's 1492 voyage, the development of a capitalist mode of production emerging from feudalism had dispossessed European peasants of independent production and subsistence agriculture. Subsequently, they

7.   Alfred W. Crosby, "The Biological Consequences of 1492", *Report on the Americas*, Vol. XXV No. 2, pg. 11.

8.   Roxanne Dunbar Ortiz, *Indians of the Americas*, Praeger Publishers, New York, 1984.

were to enter into a relationship of forced dependence to land-owners and manufacturers, leading to periods of intense class struggle, particularly as the Industrial Revolution (fueled by the expropriation of materials from the Americas and Afrika) loomed ever larger.

Indeed, the majority of Europeans who emigrated to the Americas in the 16th, 17th, and 18th centuries were impoverished merchants, petit-bourgeois traders, mercenaries, and Christian missionaries all hoping to build their fortunes in the 'New World' and escape the deepening class stratification that was quickly developing. However, the first permanent settlements were limited, their main purpose being to facilitate and maintain areas of exploitation. During the entire 16th century, only an estimated 100,000 Europeans were permanent emigrants to the Americas.

Their effects, however, were overwhelming; in the same 100-year period, the populations of the Indigenous peoples declined from 70–100 million to around 12 million. The Aztec nation alone had been reduced from around 30 million to 3 million in one 50-year period. The only term which describes this depopulation is that of Genocide; an American Indian holocaust.

Apologists for the Genocide attribute the majority of deaths to the introduction of disease epidemics such as smallpox and measles by unknowing Europeans.

While attempting to diminish the scale and intensity of the Genocide (other forms of this diminishment are claiming the population of the Americas was a much smaller portion than generally accepted demographic numbers), such a perspective disregards the conditions in which these diseases were introduced. Conditions such as wars, massacres, slavery, scorched earth policies and the subsequent destruction of subsistence agriculture and food-stocks, and the accompanying starvation, malnutrition, and dismemberment of communally-based cultures.

These conditions were not introduced by "unknowing" Europeans; they were parts of a calculated campaign based on exploitation in which the extermination of Indigenous peoples was a crucial factor.

European diseases introduced into these conditions came as an after-effect of the initial attacks. And their effects were disastrous. Once the effects of the epidemics were realized however, the use of biological warfare was also planned in the form of infected blankets and other textiles supplied to Indigenous peoples. [9]

---

9. Francis Jennings, *The Invasion of America: Indians, Colonialism, and the Cant of Conquest*, University of North Carolina Press, 1975. Jennings documents the activities of these first colonies, frequently relying on period manuscripts.

THE PENETRATION OF NORTH AMERICA

While the Spanish were destroying the Caribbean and Mesoamerican region, the Portuguese were carrying out similar campaigns in Brazil. The patterns established by the Spanish would be repeated by the Portuguese during the 16th and 17th centuries in Brazil, Uruguay, and Paraguay.

By the beginning of the 17th century, the Spanish and Portuguese had penetrated virtually every region in the southern hemisphere, establishing numerous settlements facilitated with the help of Jesuit and Franciscan missionaries, as well as mines, ranches, and plantations. Despite all this, there were still large areas in which European claims to lands remained a theoretical proposition; these areas remained outside of European control with fierce Indigenous resistance. This was particularly so in the southern regions.

During this period, French, Dutch, and advance elements of the British also established settlements in the Caribbean.

In 1604, the French occupied the island of Guadaloupe, followed by the island of Martinique and various smaller islands in the West Indies. In 1635 they occupied what is now French Guiana.

Meanwhile, the Dutch occupied a coastal region that would eventually become Surinam (Dutch Guiana) as well as settlements established by the Dutch West India Company in the area of Belize (which would later become a British colony).

The Dutch, French, and British were relatively limited in their exploits in the South Americas, and it would be in North America where their main efforts would be directed.

As has already been noted, French expeditions had penetrated the north-eastern regions of what would become Quebec and the Atlantic provinces, in the 1530s. In 1562 and 1564, the French attempted to establish settlements in South Carolina and Florida, but were driven out by the Spanish (who had claimed Florida in 1539 during de Soto's perilous expedition).

In 1585 the British also attempted settlements, on Roanoke Island in North Carolina, and again in 1586. Both attempts failed when the settlers-to-be were unable to survive.

In the period up to 1600, more reconnaissance missions were conducted; in 1576 Martin Frobisher charted the Arctic coasts encountering Inuuk, and in 1578 Francis Drake charted the coast of California.

Meanwhile, the Spanish were pushing into North America from their bases in southern Mexico, encountering resistance from Pueblos and others.

In the beginning of the 1600s, as the horse spread throughout the southwest and into the plains, Samuel de Champlain expanded on Cartier's earlier expedition, penetrating as far west as Lake Huron and Lake Ontario. His attacks on Onondago communities, using Wendat (Huron) warriors, would turn the Haudenosaunee against the French.

MEXICA EAGLE WARRIOR WITH OBSIDIAN-EDGED CLUB!

In 1606, the British finally succeeded in establishing their first permanent settlement in North America at Jamestown, Virginia. In 1620, Pilgrims (English Puritans) landed on the east coast also, establishing the Plymouth colony.

Meanwhile, Beothuks in Newfoundland had retaliated against a French attack in clashes that followed killed 37 French settlers. The French responded by arming Micmacs—traditional enemies of the Beothuks—and offering bounties for Beothuk scalps. This is believed to the origin of 'scalp-taking' by Native warriors; the stereotype of Native 'savagery' was in fact introduced by the French and, later, the Dutch. The combined attacks by the French and Micmacs led to the eventual extermination of the Beothuk nation.

In 1624, the Dutch established Fort Orange (later to become Albany, New York) and claimed the area as New Netherland.

While the Atlantic coast area of North America was becoming quickly littered with British, French and Dutch settlements, substantial differences in the lands and resources forced the focus of exploitation to differ from the colonization process underway in Meso- and South America.

In the South, the large-scale expropriation of gold and silver financed much of the invasion. As well, the dense populations of the Indigenous peoples provided a large slave-labour force to work in the first mines and plantations.

In contrast, the Europeans who began colonizing North America found a lower population density and the lands, though fertile for crops and abundant in fur-bearing animals, contained little in precious metals accessible to 17th century European technology.

The exploitation of North America was to require long-term activities which could not rely on Indigenous or Afrikan slavery but which in fact which required Indigenous participation. Maintaining colonies thousands of miles away from Europe and lacking the gold which financed the Spanish armada, the colonial forces in North America would have to rely on the gradual accumulation of agricultural products and the fur trade.

In this way, the initial settlements relied largely on the hospitality afforded them by the Native peoples. Earlier attempts at European settlements had failed for precisely this reason, as the Europeans found themselves almost completely ignorant of the land.

The growing European colonies quickly set about acquiring already cleared and cultivated land, and their expansionist policies led to fierce competition between the colonies. This bitter struggle for domination of land and trade frequently began and ended with attacks against Indigenous communities. One of the first of these 'strategic attacks' occurred in 1622 when a force from the Plymouth colony massacred a group of Pequots. In retaliation, Pequote warriors attacked a settler village at Wessagusset, which was then abandoned and subsequently absorbed into the dominion of the Plymouth colony, which had coveted the trade and land enjoyed by the Wessagusset settlers.

By 1630, the Massachusetts Bay colony had been established, and 'New England', once only a vague geographical expression, came to apply in practise to the colonies of New Plymouth, Salem, Nantucket, Rhode Island, Connecticut, New Haven and others.

The expansionist drives of the Massachusetts colonists consisted of massacres carried out against first the Pequot and eventually the Narragansetts between 1634 and 1648.

It was in this period that the transition between European dependence on Native peoples began to be reversed. Through the establishment and expansion of European colonies, increased contact with First Nations brought extensive trading, as well as disease epidemics and conflict.

Trade gradually served to break up Indigenous societies:

> Indian industry became less specialized and divided as it entered
> into closer relations of exchange with European industry. For the

> Indians, intersocietal commerce triumphed by subordinating and eliminating all crafts except those directly related to the European-Indian trade, while intertribal trading relations survived only insofar as they served the purposes of intersocietal trade. [10]

Thus, trade with European industry developed a relationship of growing dependence on the European colonists. The items traded to Natives—metal pots, knives, and occasionally rifles—were of European manufacture and supply. The trade also disrupted and changed traditional Native methods in other ways, with the introduction of alcohol and exterminationist forms of warfare—including torture—under the direction of the colonialists, as well as an overall escalation in warfare in the competition-driven fur trade and introduction of European rifles.

While disease epidemics began to spread throughout the Atlantic coastal area, the colonialists also relied to a large extent on exploiting and exaggerating already existing hostilities between First Nations, as the Spanish and Portuguese had also done in their campaigns,

> The grim epics of Cortes and Pizarro, not to speak of Columbus himself, testify to the military abilities of Spanish soldiery, but these need to be compared as well with the great failures of Narvaez, Coronado and de Soto... (The conquistadors) did not conquer Mexico and Peru unaided. Native allies were indispensable... North of New Spain, invasion started later, so Frenchmen, Dutchmen, and Englishmen found native communities...already reduced by epidemic from base populations that never approached the size of Mexico. [11]

It was at this time that the concept of treaty making began to take hold. In keeping with the English colonists early plans of keeping some level of peace with the Natives, as in 1606 when,

> the Virginia Company of London instructed its colonists to buy a stock of corn from the 'naturals' before the English intention to settle permanently should become evident. The Company's chiefs were sure that 'you cannot carry yourselves so towards them but they will grow discontented with your habitation'. [12]

---

10. Ibid, pg. 85.
11. Ibid, pg. 33.
12. Ibid, pg. 76.

The initial English (and Dutch) settlers began the process of purchasing land, supplemented as always with armed force against vulnerable Indigenous nations (such as those decimated by disease or already engaged in wars with more powerful First Nations).

It remains unclear as to what the First Nations understood of the local purchasing process, but some points are clear; there was no practise of private ownership of land, nor of selling land, among or between the Peoples prior to the arrival of the colonialists; there were however agreements and pacts between First Nations in regards to access to hunting or fishing areas. This would indicate treaties were most likely understood as agreements between First Nations and settler communities over use of certain areas of land, as well as nonaggressiveness pacts. In either case, where First Nations remained powerful enough to deter initial settler outrages the treaties were of little effect if they turned out to be less than honourable, and there was enough duplicity, fraud, and theft contained in the treaties that they could not be considered binding. Practises such as orally translating one version of a treaty and signing another on paper were frequent, as was taking European proposals in negotiations and claiming that these had been agreed upon by all—when in fact they were being negotiated. As well, violations of treaty agreements by settlers was commonplace, particularly as, for example, the Virginia colony discovered the profitability of growing tobacco (introduced to the settlers by Native peoples) and began expanding on their initial land base.

Gradually, First Nations along the Atlantic found themselves dispossessed of their lands and victims of settler depredations. One of the first conflicts that seriously threatened to drive the colonialist forces back into the sea broke out in 1622, when the Powhatan Confederacy, led by Opechancanough, attacked the Jamestown colony.

Clashes continued until 1644, when Opechancanough was captured and killed. By the mid-1600s, clashes between Natives and settlers began to increase. Tensions grew as the Europeans became more obtuse and domineering in their relationship with the First Nations. In 1655 for example, the so-called 'Peach Wars' erupted between colonialists of New Netherlands and the Delaware Nation when a Dutchman killed a Delaware woman for picking a peach tree on the colonies 'property'. The settler was subsequently killed and Delaware warriors attacked several

Dutch settlements. The fighting along the Hudson River lasted until 1664 when the Dutch forced the Delaware nation into submission by kidnapping Delaware children as hostages.

In 1675 the Narragansetts, Nipmucs, and Wapanoags, led in part by Metacom (also known as King Philip by the Europeans) rebelled against the colonies of New England following the English arrest and execution of three Wapanoags for the alleged killing of a Christianized Native, believed to be a traitor. The war ended in 1676 after the English colonialists—making use of Native allies and informers—were able to defeat the rebellion. Metacom was killed, and his family and hundreds of others sold to slavers in the West Indies. The military campaign carried out by the colonial forces decimated the Narragansett, Nipmuc, and Wapanoag nations.

Meanwhile in 1680, a Pueblo uprising led in part by the Tewa Medicine man Pope succeeded in driving out the Spanish from New Mexico. By 1689, Spanish forces were able to once again subjugate the Pueblos.

By the late 1600s, the competition between European states would dominate the colonization process in North America.

THE EUROPEAN STRUGGLE FOR HEGEMONY

Although colonial wars had been fought in the past between France, Spain, the Netherlands, and England, and conflicts had erupted between their colonies in the Americas, the late 1680s and the following 100 year period was to be a time of bitter struggle between the Europeans for domination. This period of European wars was to be played out also in the Americas, "To a great extent, the battle for colonies and the wealth they produced was the ultimate battlefield for state power in Europe." [13]

Beginning in 1689 with King William's War between the French and the English, which evolved into Queen Anne's War (1702–13), to King George's War (1744–48) and culminating in the so-called 'French and Indian War' (1754–63), the battles for colonial possessions in the Americas mirrored those raging across Europe in the same period, except that in North American and in the Caribbean, the European struggle for hegemony in the emerging world trade market would employ heavy concentrations of Native warriors.

While the British emerged victorious from the 'Great War for Empire', and the French defeated ceding Hudson Bay, Acadia, New France and other territories in a series of treaties, those who were most affected by the European struggles were the Native peoples of the Atlantic regions. The fallout from those wars was the virtual extermination of some Indigenous peoples, including the Apalachees in Florida, the establishment of colonial military garrisons and outposts, a general militarization of the region with heavier armaments and combat veterans, and the subsequent expansion of colonial settlements, extending their frontiers and pushing many First Nations further west.

During the period of the colonial wars, Indigenous resistance did not end, nor was it limited to aiding their respective 'allies'.

In 1711, the Tuscaroras attacked the English in North Carolina and fought for two years, until the English counter-insurgency campaign left hundreds dead and some 400 sold into slavery. The Tuscaroras fled north, settling among the Haudenosaunee and becoming the Sixth Nation in 1722.

---

13. Ortiz, op. cit.

In 1715, the Yamasee nation rose up against the English in South Carolina, but were virtually exterminated in a ruthless English campaign.

In 1720, the Chickasaw nation warred against French occupation, until France's capitulation to England in 1763. Similarly, Fox resistance to French colonialism continued from 1720 to around 1735.

In 1729, the Natchez nation began attacking French settlers in Louisiana after governor Sieur Chepart ordered their main village cleared for his plantations. In the ensuing battles, Chepart was killed and the French counter-insurgency campaign left the Natchez decimated, although guerrilla struggle was to continue along the Mississippi River.

In 1760 the Cherokee nation began their own guerrilla war against their 'allies' the English, in Virginia and Carolina. Led by Oconostota, the Cherokee fought for two years, eventually agreeing to a peace treaty which saw partitions of their land ceded after the English colonial forces had razed Cherokee villages and crops.

In 1761, Aleuts in Alaska attacked Russian traders following depredations on Aleut communities off the coast of Alaska (the Russian colonizers eventually moved into the Pribilof and Aleutian islands in 1797, relocating Aleuts and virtually enslaving them in the seal hunt).

Against British colonization, the Ottawa leader Pontiac led an alliance of Ottawas, Algonquins, Senecas, Mingos, and Wyandots in 1763. The offensive captured nine of twelve English garrisons and laid siege

25

to Detroit for six months. Unable to expand the insurgency or draw in promised French assistance, Pontiac eventually negotiated an end to the conflict in 1766.

Added to this period of warfare was the continuing spread of disease epidemics. In 1746 in Nova Scotia alone, 4,000 Micmacs had died of disease. With the defeat of France, the British had acquired vast regions of formerly French territory, unbeknownst to the many First Nations who lived on those lands, and with whom the French never negotiated any land treaties nor recognized any form of Native title.

At this time,

> ...the British government seized the opportunity to consolidate its imperial position by structuring formal, constitutional relations with...natives. In the Proclamation of 1763, it announced its intention of conciliating those disgruntled tribes by recognizing their land rights, by securing to them control of unceded land, and by entering into a nation-to-nation relationship. [14]

The Royal Proclamation of 1763 provided for a separate 'Indian Territory' west of the Appalachians and the original Thirteen Colonies. Within this territory there was to be no purchasing of land other than by the crown. In the colonies now under British control, including Newfoundland, Labrador, Quebec, Nova Scotia, as well as the Thirteen Colonies, settlers occupying unceded Native lands were to be removed, and private purchases of lands occupied by or reserved for Natives was prohibited—these lands could only be purchased by the crown in the presence of the First Nations.

As grand as these statements were, they were routinely violated by colonialists and rarely enforced. Indeed, one year following the proclamation, Lord Dunmore—the governor of the Virginia colony—had already breached the demarcation line by granting to veterans of the 'French and Indian War' who had served under him lands which were part of the Shawnee nation. The Shawnee retaliation was not short in coming, but Dunmore's challenge to British control was to precipitate in form and substance another period of conflict that would see the colonization process expand westward. And that period of conflict would underline the real intent of the Royal Proclamation as a strategic document in the defense of British colonial interests in North America.

---

14. John S. Milloy, "The Early Indian Acts: Developmental Strategy and Constitutional Change", *As Long As The Sun Shines and Water Flows*, University of BC Press, 1983, pg. 56.

TRAGEDY: THE UNITED STATES IS CREATED

With the dominance of British power on a world scale, the European struggle for hegemony in the Americas was nearing its end. Subsequently, the 18th and 19th centuries were to be a period of wars for independence that would force the European states out of the Americas. Foremost among these wars was the independence struggle that would lead to the birth of the United States.

Emerging from the 'Great War for Empire', Britain found itself victorious but also heavily in debt. To defray the cost of maintaining and defending the colonies, Britain substantially changed its colonial policies. Large portions of the financial costs of the colonies were placed directly on the colonies themselves through a series of taxes. The imposition of the taxes incited the settlers to demand taxes be imposed only with their consent. In fact, the question of taxes was part of a wider debate about who should control and profit from colonialism, the colonies or the colonial centres.

By 1775, settler protests and revolts had culminated in a general war for independence that continued until 1783, when the British capitulated and ceded large portions of its territories along the Atlantic.

That the British colonial forces did not lose more territory can be attributed much to the participation of numerous First Nations on the side of the British; the Royal Proclamation was thus a strategy to dampen Native resistance to British colonialism (as in the eruption of King George's War in 1744 when Micmacs allied themselves with the French and, following the Treaty of Aix-la-Chapelle in 1748, continued fighting the British, who then concluded a treaty of "Peace and Friendship" with the Micmacs), as well as a method of forming military alliances with First Nations, if not at least their neutrality in European conflicts.

As in previous European struggles, Indigenous peoples were used as expendable troops, and the extensive militarization further consolidated settler control,

> The end of the war saw thousands of Whites, United Empire Loyalists, flock to Nova Scotia. They came in such numbers and spread so widely over the Maritime region that it was considered

27

necessary to divide Nova Scotia into three provinces to ease administrative problems; New Brunswick, Cape Breton, Nova Scotia...and Ile St.-Jean, soon to be renamed Prince Edward Island. [15]

To the south, the rebellious settlers were establishing their newly-created United States. For the First Nations in this region, the war had been particularly destructive; the colonial rebels had carried out scorched-earth campaigns against the Shawnee, Delaware, Cherokee, and the Haudenosaunee (who had suffered a split with the Oneidas and Tuscaroras allying themselves with the revolutionaries). Here again the Royal Proclamation remained a useful tool in reinforcing the British colonial frontier and retaining Native allies,

> Adherence to the principles of the...Proclamation...remained the basis of Britain's Indian policy for more than half a century, and explains the success of the British in maintaining the Indians as allies in Britain's wars in North America... Even when Britain lost much of its North American territory after 1781, and its Indian allies lost their traditional lands as a result of their British alliance, the Crown purchased land from the Indians living within British territory and gave it to their allies who moved north... [16]

Having consolidated the Thirteen Colonies along the Atlantic seaboard, the independent United States quickly set about expanding westward, launching military campaigns to extend the frontiers of settlement.

One of the first of these campaigns began in 1790 under the order of President George Washington. Consisting of about 1,100 Pennsylvania, Virginia, and Kentucky militiamen led by Brigadier General Josiah Harmar, the force was quickly defeated by a confederacy of Miami, Shawnee, Ojibway, Delaware, Potawatomi, and Ottawa warriors led by the Miami chief Michikinikwa (Little Turtle). A second force was dispatched and defeated in November, 1791. Finally, in 1794, a large force led by General Anthony Wayne defeated the confederacy, now led by Turkey Foot, near the shores of Lake Erie. Warriors who survived made their way to the British Fort Miami garrison. But the British—former allies of many of the First Nations in the confederacy during the revolutionary war—refused them shelter, and hundreds were slaughtered at the gates

---

15. George F. G. Stanley, "As Long as the Sun Shines and the Water Flows: An Historical Comment", ibid. pg. 5–6.

16. John L. Tobias, "Protection, Civilization, Assimilation: An Outline History of Canada's Indian Policy", ibid. pg. 40.

by Wayne's soldiers. Although the confederacy was essentially broken, the Miami would continue armed resistance up to 1840.

The 'Indian Wars' launched by the U.S. continued for the next 100 years, following an exterminationist policy that was aimed at destroying Native nations and securing those remnants who survived in (what was then believed) barren and desolate reserves. Once the People were contained in these Bantustans, the next step was the destruction of Native culture under the auspices of then-emerging governmental agencies.

As the U.S. moved to a higher level of war against First Nations, it also began moving against competing European powers still present in the Americas.

Tecumseh

In 1812, using the pretext of Native raids along its northern frontier from British territories, U.S. forces attempted to invade British North America. Here again, Britain's colonial policies proved effective; an alliance of Native nations (who had their own interests in full implementation of the 1763 Proclamation) and European settlers succeeded in repulsing the U.S. expansion. Among those who fought against the U.S. invasion were the Native leaders Tecumseh—a Shawnee chief who worked to form a Native confederacy against the Europeans (and who argued that no one individual or grouping could sell the lands, as it belonged to all the Native peoples); Black Hawk—a leader of the Sauk who would also lead future Native insurgencies; and Joseph Brant—a leader in the Haudenosaunee who was rewarded with a large territory by the British and promptly began selling off partitions to European settlers (in history, he is regarded as a "hero" by Euro-Americans but a traitor by his people). Tecumseh was killed in battle in the Battle of Moraviantown in Ontario in 1813.

In 1815, hostilities between Britain and the U.S. were formally ended in the Treaty of Ghent, though neither the U.S. war on Natives, or Native resistance, subsided.

REVOLUTIONS IN THE "NEW WORLD"

Following the American Revolution, movements for independence began breaking out in South and Central America.

Despite the seemingly monolithic appearance of Spanish or Portuguese colonialism in the first three centuries following the European invasion, and despite the genocidal policies of the conquistadors, Native resistance continued. Particularly in, for example, the interior region of the Yucatan Peninsula, the lowland forests of Peru, the Amazon region, and even in the Andean highlands—which had suffered such a severe depopulation; between 1532 and 1625, the population of the Andean peoples is estimated to have declined from 9 million to 700,000. In these regions, colonial domination was continually challenged and formed the base for resistance movements that began even in the 1500s.

Among the first of these revolts was the Vilacabamba rebellion of 1536 led by Manqu Inka. Although the insurgency was unable to expand and failed to drive the Spanish out, the rebels were able to establish a "liberated zone" in the Vilacabamba region of present-day Bolivia for the next three decades. [17] The ending of the initial revolt is recognized as the execution of another leader, Tupac Amaru I in 1572.

Other major insurgencies also broke out in Ecuador in 1578, 1599, and 1615. The Itza of Tayasal in the Yucatan Peninsula remained unsubjugated until 1697.

"Europeans found it particularly difficult to establish effective transportation and communication facilities in the forest lowlands of the Maya area... Though the Spaniards achieved formal sovereignty over Yucatan with relative ease, many local Maya groups successfully resisted effective domination...for centuries." [18]

---

17. Silvia Rivera Cusicanqui, "Aymara Past, Aymara Future", *Report on the Americas*, Vol. XXV No. 3, pg. 20.
18. John S. Henderson, *The World of the Ancient Maya*, Cornell University Press, 1981, pg. 32.

Keeping pace with colonial developments in North America, the Spanish introduced a series of laws in the 17th century known as the Leyes de Indias. Similar to the later 1763 Proclamation introduced in British North America, the laws partitioned the Andean region into a 'Republic of Spain' and a 'Republic of Indians'—each with its own separate courts, laws and rights. The Leyes de Indias were, "from the point of view of the colonial state...a pragmatic measure to prevent the extermination of the [Indigenous] labour force..."[19]

Despite its seeming "liberalism", forced labour accompanied by tax laws remained in place, and the regulation was never fully enforced.

In 1742, Juan Santos Atahualpa led an Indigenous resistance movement in Peru comprised largely of Yanesha (Amuesha) and Ashaninka (Campa) peoples that fought off Spanish colonization for more than a century.

In the 18th century, Indigenous resistance broke out in a major revolt in the colony of Upper Peru (now Bolivia), led by Jose Gabriel Tupac Amaru.

> Much has been written about the 1780 Indian rebellion led by Jose Gabriel Tupaq Amaru and his successors; less is known about the Chayanta and Sikasika revolts which occurred at the same time, the latter led by Julian Apasa Tupaq Katari. For more than half a century, colonial tax laws had provoked a groundswell of protest... In mid-1780, an apparently spontaneous revolt broke out in Macha, in the province of Chayanta, to free an Indian cacique, Tomas Katari, jailed after a dispute with local mestizo authorities... Then in November 1780, Jose Gabriel Tupaq Amaru led a well-organized rebellion in Tungasuca, near Cuzco. Julian Apasa Tupaq Katari, an Indian commoner from Sullkaw (Sikasika) rose up and laid siege to La Paz from March to October 1781 during which one fourth of the city's population died. After the defeat in April 1781 of Tupaq Amaru in Cuzco, the rebellion shifted to Azangaro, where his relatives Andres and Diego Cristobal led the struggle. Andres successfully laid siege to Sorata in August of that year, but by November he and Diego Cristobal were forced to surrender to the Spanish authorities. The rebellion was crushed by the beginning of 1782.[20]

The leaders, perceived or real, were captured and executed; they were quartered, decapitated, or burned alive.

---

19. Sylvia Rivera Cusicanqui, op. cit.
20. Ibid. pg. 21.

While Indigenous resistance continued and frequently sent shock-waves throughout the ranks of the colonialists—including Spaniards and Creoles (descendants of Spanish settlers in the Americas)—the colonies themselves began to experience movements for independence comprised of Creoles and Mestizos.

The backgrounds to the movements for independence—like in the U.S.—are found in the oppressive taxation and monopolistic trade laws imposed by the colonial centers, both of which constrained the economic growth of the colonies. As well, Creoles were generally by-passed for colonial positions which went to agents born in Spain.

The first major settler revolt was in 1809 in the colony of Upper Peru (Bolivia), which succeeded in temporarily overthrowing Spanish authorities. In 1810 Colombia declared its independence, followed one year later by Venezuela. In 1816, Argentina declared its independence, and the next year General Jose de San Martin led troops across the Andes to "liberate Chile and Peru from the Royalist forces". Wars for independence spread quickly, and Spanish royalist forces lost one colony after another in decisive conflicts, culminating in the Battle of Ayacucho in 1824 in Peru, which effectively diminished Spain's domination in the Americas (which was already dampened by Napoleon's invasion of Spain in the same period).

Although the independence movements succeeded in overthrowing Spanish and Portuguese forces, they were led by, and in the interests of, Creole elites—with the assistance of land-owners and merchants,

> ...the revolutions for independent state formation in the Americas in the late 18th and early 19th centuries must be seen as being in the mode of European nation-state formation for the purpose of capitalist development. Although they were anti-'mother country', they were not anti-colonial (just as the formation of Rhodesia and South Africa as states were not anticolonial events). [21]

The present-day Confederation of Indigenous Nationalities of Ecuador (CONAIE) describes the independence of Ecuador, for example, as

> not mean(ing) any change in our living conditions; it was nothing more than the passage of power from the hands of the Spaniards to the hands of the Creoles. [22]

---

21. Roxanne Dunbar Ortiz, op. cit.
22. Quoted in Les Field, "Ecuador's Pan-Indian Uprising", *Report on the Americas*, Vol. XXV No. 3, pg. 41.

As in the U.S. example, the newly-independent states quickly set about consolidating their positions politically and militarily and pursuing economic expansion.

The result was an eruption of wars between the independent states over borders, trade, and ultimately for resources. In 1884 the War of the Pacific began, involving Bolivia, Chile, and Peru in a dispute over access to nitrate resource. From 1865–70, Argentina, Brazil, and Uruguay allied themselves against Paraguay in the bloody War of the Triple Alliance—a war in which Paraguay lost a large amount of its male population—primarily Guarani.

As in North America, these and other conflicts most adversely affected the First Nations peoples. The majority of those who died in the War of the Triple Alliance were Native. As well, the militarization that occurred created large reserves of well-equipped, combat-experienced troops. In Argentina and Chile, these military reserves were directed against invading then unsubjugated regions where Mapuche resistance had persisted for centuries. Between 1865 and 1885, a militarized frontier existed from which attacks against the Mapuche were conducted. Tens of thousands of Mapuche were killed, the survivors dispersed to reservation areas.

In the 1870s, the development of vulcanization in Europe led to an invasion of the Upper Amazon regions of Brazil, Colombia, Ecuador, Peru, and Bolivia—where rubber trees would eventually supply the world market. In the Putumayo river region of northern Peru and Colombia alone, 40,000 Natives were killed between 1886 and 1919 (by 1920, it's estimated that the depopulation of the rubber areas had reached 95% in some areas). [23]

It was in this post-independence period that—arising from the complete transition from Feudalism to capitalism in Europe—new forms of European domination were being introduced. Briefly, this consisted of the introduction of bank loans directed primarily at developing infrastructures for the export of raw and manufactured materials: roads, railways, and ports, particularly in the mining and agricultural industries. In the 1820s, English banks loaned over 21 million pounds to former Spanish colonies. Through the debts, and the subsequent import of European technology and machinery necessary for large-scale mining and agribusiness—necessary to begin repayment of the loans—dependence

---

23.   Andrew Gray, "The Amerindians of South America", *Minority Rights Group Report* No. 15, London, 1987, pg. 8.

was gradually established (and continues today in the form of the International Monetary Fund and the World Bank, controlled by the G-7). [24]

During the same period, the U.S. was also setting footholds in the region. In 1853, five years after gold was discovered in previously unknown areas in Central America, U.S. marines invaded Nicaragua. In 1898, following the Spanish-American War, Puerto Rico and Cuba were annexed to the U.S. (Puerto Rico remains today as the last U.S. colonial nation). As well, U.S. forces occupied the Philippines—carrying out massacres of men, women, and children—and Hawaii came under U.S. control in 1893. With these actions the U.S. established itself as an emerging capitalist power, and the eventual extent of U.S. imperialism was beginning to take shape.

On a global scale, the development of imperialism had now established itself internationally; the full division of the world between predominantly European powers and the U.S. was complete (and would subsequently lead to two world wars).

---

24. G-7: the grouping of the seven most advanced industrialized countries at the time: Britain, Canada, France, Italy, Germany, Japan, and the USA. In 1998 the Group was joined by Russia, and is now known as the G-8. The Group meets annually to determine world economic policies; together they hold dominant positions in the world economic order.

MANIFEST DESTINY AND THE U.S. INDIAN WARS

While the U.S. was in the process of establishing itself as an imperialist world power, it was still struggling to consolidate itself as a continental base and countering armed resistance by First Nations.

Prior to the U.S.-British War of 1812, Louisiana was purchased from France, in 1803, and Spain had ceded Florida in 1819. By 1824, the Bureau of Indian Affairs was organized as part of the War Department. Military campaigns were launched against First Nations, from the Shawnee of the Mississippi Valley to the Seminole in Florida. At the same time, the legalistic instruments for occupation were being introduced. In 1830 the Indian Removal Act was implemented, and in 1834 Congress reorganized the various departments dealing with Indian repression by creating the U.S.

Tatanka Yotanka (Sitting Bull)

Department of Indian Affairs, and the Indian Trade and Intercourse Act which redefined the 'Indian Territory' and 'Permanent Indian Frontier'. The 'Indian Territory' had been previously defined in 1825 as lands west of the Mississippi. Following the formation of the territories of Wisconsin and Iowa, the frontier was extended from the Mississippi to the 95th meridian.

The Indian Removal Act was directed at forced relocation of Natives east of the 95th meridian to the west of it. In 1838, U.S. troops forced thousands of

Cherokee into concentration camps, from which they were forced westward on the Trail of Tears. In the midst of winter, one out of every four Cherokees died from cold, hunger, or diseases. Many other nations were forcibly relocated: the Choctaws, Chickasaws, Creeks, Shawnees, Miamis, Ottawas, Wendats and Delawares. The 'Permanent Indian Frontier' was a militarized line of U.S. garrisons, similar to that in Argentina and Chile during the same period.

But the 'Indian Frontier' was not to hold. Like the British Royal Proclamation of 1763, the restrictions on Europeans settling or trading in these regions were routinely ignored. With the U.S. annexation of northern Mexico in 1848, the U.S. acquired the territories of Texas, California, New Mexico, Arizona, Utah and Colorado. The same year, gold was discovered in California. With these two events, the large-scale invasion of the 'Indian Territory' was underway. Under the ideology of Manifest Destiny, the U.S. was to launch a renewed period of genocidal war against those regions and First Nations which remained unsubjugated. The theatre of war extended from the Great Lakes region around Minnesota, south of the Rio Grande, and west to California, extending north to Washington state. It was a period of war which involved many First Nations: the Lakota, Cheyenne, Commanche, Kiowa, Yakima, Nez Perce, Walla Walla, Cayuse, Arapaho, Apache, Navajo, Shoshone, Kickapoos, and many others. It was also a war from which many Native leaders would leave a legacy of struggle that, like those struggles in South and Mesoamerica, would remain as symbols of resistance to the European colonization: Crazy Horse, Tatanka Yotanka (Sitting Bull), Ten Bears, Victorio, Geronimo, Quanah Parker, Wovoka, Black Kettle, Red Cloud, Chief Joseph, and so many others.

Although the 'Indian Wars' of this period were by no means one-sided—the U.S. forces suffered many defeats—the U.S. colonial forces succeeded in gradually and ruthlessly gaining dominance. Various factors contributed to this, following the patterns of previous campaigns against Native peoples: the continuing spread of diseases such as measles, smallpox, and cholera (between 1837–70, at least four major smallpox epidemics swept through the western plains, and between 1850–60 a cholera epidemic hit the Great Basin and southern plains); the use of informers and traitors; and the overwhelming strength of U.S. forces in both weaponry and numbers of soldiers. Combined with outright treachery and policies of extermination, these factors continued to erode the strength of once-powerful First Nations.

One of the major turning points in this period can be seen as the U.S. Civil War.

AFRIKAN SLAVERY, AFRIKAN REBELLION, AND THE U.S. CIVIL WAR

Ostensibly a moral crusade to "abolish slavery", the U.S. Civil War of 1861–65 was in reality a conflict between the commercial and industrial development of the North against the agrarian stagnation based on Afrikan peoples' slave labour of the South.

By the 19th century, 10 to 15 million Afrikan peoples had been relocated to the Americas by first Portuguese, then English, Spanish, and U.S. colonialists.

These peoples came from all regions of Afrika: Senegal, the Ivory Coast, Angola, Mozambique, etc.—and from many Afrikan Nations: the Yoruba, Kissi, Senefu, Foulah, Fons, Adjas, and many others.

Enslaved, these peoples were forced to labour in the mines, textile mills, factories, and plantations that served first the European markets and, after the wars for independence, the newly-created nation-states of the Americas.

The slave-trade in both American and Afrikan Indigenous peoples was absolutely necessary for the European colonization of the Americas. The forced relocation of millions of Afrikan peoples also introduced new dynamics into the colonization process, not only in the economics of European occupation, but also in the development of Afrikan peoples' resistance.

As early as 1526, Afrikan slaves had rebelled in a short-lived Spanish colony in South Carolina, and after their escape took refuge amongst First Nations peoples. In the Caribbean and South America,

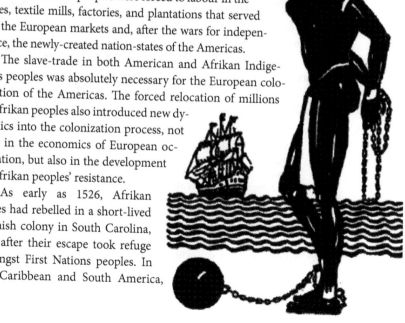

where Afrikan slavery was first centered, large revolts frequently broke out and escaped Afrikan slaves took refuge amongst Caribs and Arawaks. In Northeast Brazil, an Afrikan rebellion succeeded in organizing the territory of Palmares—which grew to one-third the size of Portugal.

Probably one of the most famous Afrikan and Native alliances was the example of the escaped Afrikan slaves and the Seminole in Florida. The escaped Afrikans had "formed liberated Afrikan communities as a semi-autonomous part of the sheltering Seminole Nation". [25] Together, these two peoples would carry out one of the strongest resistance struggles against the U.S. The so-called Seminole Wars began in 1812 when Georgia vigilantes attempted to recapture Afrikans for enslavement, and continued for thirty years under the U.S. campaign of relocations. The Seminole Wars, under the fanatical direction of President Jackson, were the most costly of the U.S. 'Indian Wars'; over 1,600 U.S. soldiers were killed and thousands wounded at the cost of some $30 million. Even after this, the Seminole-Afrikan guerrillas remained unsubjugated. The solidarity between the Afrikans and the Seminoles is most clear in the second Seminole War of 1835. The Seminoles, under Osceola, refused to accept relocation to Oklahoma—one of the key disagreements also being the U.S. insistence on separation of the Afrikans from their Seminole brothers and sisters. The U.S. forces relaunched their war, and were never able to achieve a clear victory.

By the mid-1800s, slavery was viewed by some parts of the U.S. ruling class as an obstacle to economic growth and expansion. The anti-slavery campaign, led by the North, was a practical effort to free land and labour from the limitations of the closed system of plantation agriculture based on slave labour;

> Slavery had become an obstacle to both the continued growth of settler society and the interests of the Euro-Amerikan bourgeoisie. It was not that slavery was unprofitable itself. It was, worker for worker, much more profitable than white wagelabour. Afrikan slaves in industry cost the capitalists less than one-third the wages of white workingmen... But the American capitalists needed to greatly expand their labour force. While the planters believed that importing new millions of Afrikan slaves would most profitably meet this need, it was clear that this would only

---

25.   J. Sakai, *Settlers: The Myth of the White Proletariat*, Morningstar Press, 1989, pg. 27.

add fuel to the fires of the already insurrectionary Afrikan colony. Profit had to be seen not only in the squeezing of a few more dollars on a short-term, individual basis, but in terms of the needs of an entire Empire and its future. And it was not just the demand for labour alone that outmoded the slave system. Capitalism needed giant armies of settlers, waves and waves of new European shock-troops to help conquer and hold new territory, to develop it for the bourgeoisie and garrison it against the oppressed. [26]

The "insurrectionary fires" had already dealt the occupation forces a shocking blow in 1791 in the Haitian Revolution. Afrikan slaves, led in part by Toussaint L'Ouverture, rebelled and defeated Spanish, English, and French forces, establishing the Haitian Republic that offered citizenship to any Native or Afrikan peoples who wanted it.

There were also increasing revolts within the U.S., including the 1800 revolt in Virginia led by Gabriel Prosser, and Nat Turner's revolt in 1831 which killed sixty settlers."The situation became more acute as the developing capitalist economy created trends of urbanization and industrialization. In the early 1800s the Afrikan population of many cities was rising faster than that of Euro-Americans." [27] The revolts led by Gabriel and Turner had caused discussions in the Virginia legislature on ending slavery, and public rallies had been held in Western Virginia demanding an all white Virginia.

Combined, these factors led the North to agitate for an end to slavery as one specific form of exploitation. In turn, the Southern states, led by plantation owners and slavers, threatened to secede from the Union. The Civil War began.

---

26. Ibid, pg. 25.
27. Ibid, pg. 31.

BLACK RECONSTRUCTION AND DECONSTRUCTION

The beginning of the U.S. Civil War in 1861 posed various problems for the northern Union ruling class. Not only was the war for the preservation of an expanding continental empire, but it also opened up a second front: that of a liberation struggle by enslaved Afrikan peoples. With a population of four million, the rising of these Afrikans in the South proved crucial in the defeat of the Confederacy. By the tens of thousands, Afrikan slaves escaped from the slavers and enlisted in the Union forces. This massive withdrawal of slave-labour hit the Southern economy hard, and the Northern forces were bolstered by the thousands.

Towards the end of the War in 1865, those Afrikans who did not escape began a large-scale strike following the defeat of the Confederacy. They claimed the lands that they had laboured on, and began arming themselves—not only against the Southern planters but also against the Union army. Widespread concerns about this 'dangerous position' of Afrikans in the South led to 'Black Reconstruction'; Afrikans were promised democracy, human rights, self-government and popular ownership of the land. In reality, it was a strategy for returning Euro-American dominance involving:

1. The military repression of the most organized and militant Afrikan communities.

2. Pacifying the Afrikan peoples by neocolonialism, using elements of the Afrikan petit-bourgeoisie to lead their people into embracing U.S. citizenship as the answer to all problems. Instead of nationhood and liberation, the neo-colonial agents told the masses that their democratic demands could be met by following the Northern settler capitalists... [28]

---

28.   Ibid, pg. 39.

Following this strategy, Union army forces attacked Afrikan communities who were occupying land, forcing tens of thousands off collectively held land and arresting the "leaders". Afrikan troops who had fought in the Union army were quickly disarmed and dispersed, or sent to fight as colonial troops in the ongoing "Indian Wars". White supremacist terrorist organizations formed, one of the most infamous—but not the only—being the Ku Klux Klan.

Under the 14th Amendment to the U.S. Constitution, Afrikans became U.S. citizens, including the right to vote. Through the neo-colonialist strategy of Reconstruction, Afrikans were able to push through reforms including integrated juries, protective labour reforms, divorce and property rights for women, and an involvement in local government.

However, even these small reforms were too much for Southern Whites. Reconstruction was vigorously resisted—not only by former slaves and planters but also by poor Whites who flocked to organizations such as the KKK, White Caps, White Cross, and the White League. Thousands of Afrikans were killed during state elections as the White supremacist groups conducted terrorist campaigns aimed at countering the gains of Reconstruction and preserving White supremacy.

> In 1876–77, the final accommodation between Northern capital and the Southern planters was reached in the 'Hayes-Tilden deal'. The South promised to accept the dominance of the Northern bourgeoisie over the entire Empire, and to permit the Republican candidate Rutherford B. Hayes to succeed Grant in the U.S. Presidency. In return, the Northern bourgeoisie agreed to let the planters have regional hegemony over the South, and to withdraw the last of the occupying Union troops so that the Klan could take care of the Afrikans as they wished. While the guarded remnants of Reconstruction held out here and there for some years (Afrikan Congressmen were elected from the South until 1895), the critical year of 1877 marked their conclusive defeat. [29]

Not insignificantly during this same period, Northern working class Whites were engaged in a vicious class struggle for an 8 hour work day, even as Afrikans were under attack by the KKK and other racist organizations. And, at the same time, little notice was made of the military extermination campaigns being carried out against Native peoples.

---

29.   Ibid, pg. 41.

During the War, many First Nations attempted to remain "neutral" in the South, although some promises by the Confederacy for land stimulated some First Nations to side with the South. But "neutrality" is not the same as passive; Native peoples continued their own resistance to colonization. From 1861–63 the Apaches led by Cochise and Mangas Colorado fought occupation forces, a resistance that would continue until 1886 when Geronimo was captured. The Santee also engaged the U.S. military from 1862–63 led by Little Crow. In 1863–64, this war would shift to North Dakota under the Teton. In 1863, the Western Shoshone fought settlers and attacked military patrols and supply routes in Utah and Idaho. That same year, the Navajo rebelled in New Mexico and Arizona.

With the completion of the transcontinental railroad in 1869, settlement of the West increased rapidly. The militarization from the Civil War, and the ability to supply and facilitate large-scale military operations, opened up the final period in the "Indian Wars". In the post-Civil War period, the genocidal process of colonization was to enter a new phase, even at the price of thousands of U.S. troops dead and wounded, and each dead Indian coming at the price of $1 million. By 1885, the last great herd of buffalo would be slaughtered by Euro-American hunters—this also forming a part of the counter-insurgency strategy of depriving the Plains Indians of their primary food source. Five years later, 350 Lakotas would be massacred at Chankpe Opi Wakpala, the creek called Wounded Knee.

THE COLONIZATION OF CANADA

In contrast to the U.S. campaign of extermination, the colonization process in Canada lacked the large-scale military conflicts that characterized the U.S. "Indian Wars". Although many Euro-Canadians[30] would like to believe that these differences in colonization lie in fundamentally different values, cultures, etc., they are no more than the result of differences in colonial practises rooted in basic economic needs and strategies. As can be seen in the aftermath of the U.S. War for Independence, there followed a period of rapid expansion and settlement. Following the consolidation of the "13 British colonies along the North Atlantic, and armed with a pre-imperialist thrust (the Monroe

Doctrine and the ideology of 'manifest destiny'), the entrepreneurs controlling the new state machinery dispatched their military forces rapidly across North America". [31]

Canada, on the other hand, did not fight a war for independence and remained firmly a part of the British Empire.

As previously discussed, the first major colonization of what would become eastern "Canada" was carried out by France. Between 1608 and 1756, some 10,000 French settlers had arrived in Canada. The "French

---

30. Euro-Canadian: a term used to distinguish between descendants of Europeans in the U.S. and those in Canada.
31. Ortiz, op. cit.

and Indian Wars" of the 18th century resulted in the defeat of the French forces; the subsequent Treaty of 1763 established British rule over New France (now Quebec). With the Quebec Act of 1774, the province of Quebec was expanded, British criminal law established, and the feudal administration implemented by France remained largely unchanged. Conflicts related to civil matters and property remained regulated under French civil law. The seigneurial system, a feudal system in which the land of the province was given in grant from the King to seigneurs (usually lower nobility and from the Church), who, in turn, rented the land to peasants in return for an annual rent (called tithes, payable in goods of products raised on the land), was continued. As with the 1763 Royal Proclamation, the Quebec Act secured the loyalty of the French clergy and aristocracy in the U.S. War for Independence.

As a result of the wars of the 18th century, French settlement had grown to 60,000 as soldiers employed by France swelled the French population. The expansion of the province under the Quebec Act had seized a large portion of the "Indian territory" and placed it under Crown jurisdiction. Following the U.S. War for Independence, some 40,000 loyalists fled the former British colonies and settled in Canada, occupying more Native lands—particularly that of the Haudenosaunee. British colonial authorities went to some lengths to acquire land while placating the still geo-militarily important Indians. [32]

While the colonialists were busy consolidating the administration of "British North America", the Pacific Northwest was coming under increased reconnaissance.

Beginning in 1774, the first recorded colonizers into the area of British Columbia came aboard the Spanish ship Santiago. Four years later, an expedition led by James Cook descended upon the area, leading to the establishment of a large and profitable fur trade. The dominance of the fur trade

---

32. Negotiations with the Mississaugas of southern Ontario were conducted as early as 1781, providing land for communities from the Haudenosaunee, whose lands were supplied to British loyalists in a strategic defensive line along the U.S. border. Between 1781 and 1836, 23 such land cessions were conducted. Not treaties but instead "simple real estate deals" in which the British paid with goods and later money. In 1818 the practise was adopted of paying annuities. By 1830 these annual payments were directed at building houses and purchasing farm equipment—in line with changing colonial practises. "This was then followed by the establishment of the band fund system", see As Long as the Sun Shines, op. cit., pg. 9.

would last until around 1854 when European settlement began to increase rapidly along with the mining and logging industries. As a result of the early dominance of the fur trade, which relied on Native collaboration, British colonizers curtailed their military operations. Nevertheless, conflicts did erupt, primarily against British depredations. As more ships frequented the area, clashes spread with attacks on colonial vessels and the shelling of Native villages.

Even before European settlement in BC, the impact of the traders was disastrous. For example, from 1835 when the first census was taken of the Kwakwaka'wakw nation, to 1885, there was between a 70 to 90 percent reduction in population (from around 10,700 to 3,000). [33] In an all too familiar pattern, the intrusion of European traders had set into motion disease epidemics, even as early as the 1780s and '90s. In 1836, a smallpox epidemic hit the northern coast, and the fur trade was "depressed all that winter and the following spring". [34] Following an invasion of gold hunters into the region in 1858, one of the most devastating epidemics struck in 1862, killing at least 20,000 Indians. [35]

Meanwhile, in British North America, the geo-military importance of the First Nations was quickly being eroded. With the influx of loyalists after the U.S. War for Independence, the European population had grown and was strategically garrisoned

Lil'Wat nation protestor, British Columbia

---

33. Dara Culhane Speck, *An Error in Judgement*, Talonbooks, Vancouver, 1987, pg. 72.
34. Wilson Duff, "The Indian History of BC, Vol. 1: The Impact of the White Man". *Anthropology in BC*, Memoir No. 5, 1964. BC Provincial Museum, Victoria 1965 (First Edition), pg. 42.
35. Ibid, pg. 42–43.

in key military areas—conflicts with the U.S. were predicted. As well as further increasing the European population in the region, the War of 1812 and U.S. policies of moving Natives from the northern frontier had broken up confederacies and greatly diminished the power of the First Nations in the area. After this, British colonial policies changed from essentially forming military alliances to a higher level of colonization through policies of breaking down the collective power of First Nations. Christianization and an overall Europeanization of Native peoples was developed as official policy. By the 1850s, an instrument had been created to this end: "The Gradual Civilization Act of 1857".

> The Act was based upon the assumption that the full civilization of the tribes could be achieved only when Indians were brought into contact with individualized property... Any Indian...adjudged by a special board of examiners to be educated, free from debt, and of good moral character could on application be awarded twenty hectares of land... [36]

Here, the "civilization of the tribes" should be read as the elimination of the basis of Native cultures and de facto the First Nations as nations. The twenty hectares of land were to be taken from the reserve land base, subsequently breaking up the collective and communitarian land practises of Native peoples and replacing these with individual parcels of land; all the easier, from the viewpoint of the colonizer, to achieve the long-term goal of completely eliminating First Nations as nations and leaving nothing but dispersed, acculturated, peoples to be assimilated into European society. The patriarchal dimensions of forced-assimilation were also clear: only males could be so enfranchised.[37] A Commission of Inquiry had further recommended that reserve lands be restricted to a maximum of 25 acres per family, and that Native organization be gradually replaced with a municipal form of government.

At the same time, new methods in acquiring land were developed. Beginning in 1850 and continuing into the 20th century, a series of treaties were "negotiated" in which Native nations ceded immense tracts of land in return for reserve land, hunting and fishing rights, education, medical care, and the payment of annuities. The first such treaties were the Robinson treaties, which would be renegotiated in 1871 as Treaties No. 1 and No. 2.

---

36. John S. Milloy, op. cit., pg. 58.
37. Kathleen Jamieson, *Indian Women and the Law in Canada: Citizens Minus*, Advisory Council on the Status of Women, Indian Rights for Indian Women, Canada, 1978, pg. 27–28.

The relationship between the immediate requirements of the internal imperialist expansion and the treaties is remarkable. The first of these treaties was sought, according to a 19th century historian's first-hand report, 'in consequence of the discovery of minerals on the shores of Lake Huron and Superior'... The prairie treaties were obtained immediately in advance of agricultural settlement, and the treaty which includes parts of the Northwest Territories was negotiated immediately upon the discovery of oil in the Mackenzie Valley. [38]

While the colonizers knew what they wanted in proposing the treaties, Native peoples were unprepared for the duplicity and dishonour of the treaty-seekers. When a commission journeyed to the Northwest Territories to investigate unfulfilled provisions of Treaties 8 and 11, they found that

At a number of meetings, Indians who claimed to have been present at the time when the Treaties were signed stated that they definitely did not recall hearing about the land entitlement in the Treaties. They explained that poor interpreters were used and their chiefs and head men had signed even though they did not know what the Treaties contained. [39]

The treaties were important aspects of the plan for the expansion of Canada westward and economic development based on resource extraction and agriculture. Indeed, the Confederation of Canada in the British North America Act of 1867 was aimed primarily at consolidating the then-existing eastern provinces and facilitating in this westward expansion; the primary instruments of this were the trans-Canada railway, telegraph lines, and roads. This expansion was seen not only as economically necessary but also politically urgent as the U.S. was expanding westward at the same time.

The invasion of the prairie regions was not without conflict. The most significant resistance in this period was that of the Metis peoples—descendants of primarily French and Scottish settlers and Cree—in what would become Manitoba. The Red River Rebellion, also known as the First Riel rebellion after Louis Riel, a Metis leader, erupted following an influx of Euro-Canadian settlers and the purchase of the territory from the controlling Hudsons Bay Company, by the government

38. Donald R. Colborne, Norman Ziotkin, "Internal Canadian Imperialism and the Native People", *Imperialism, Nationalism, and Canada*, Marxist Institute of Toronto, Between the Lines and New Hogtown Press, 1987, pg. 164.
39. Ibid, pg. 167. Quote from Report of the Commission appointed to investigate the unfulfilled provisions of Treaties 8 and 11 as they apply to the Indians of the Mackenzie District, 1959, pgs. 3–4.

of Canada. The rebellion was directed against the annexation of the territory over the Metis—who numbered some 10,000 in the region. A force of 400 armed Metis seized a small garrison and demanded democratic rights for the Metis in the Confederation. The following year the Manitoba Act made the territory a province. However, fifteen years later in 1885 the Metis along with hundreds of Cree warriors under the chiefs Big Bear and Opetecahanawaywin (Poundmaker) were again engaged in widespread armed resistance against colonization. For almost four months the resistance continued against thousands of government troops which, unlike in 1870, were now transported quickly and en masse on the new Canadian Pacific railway. After several clashes the Metis and Cree warriors were eventually defeated; the Cree and Metis guerrillas imprisoned, killed in battles or executed. Another Metis leader, Gabriel Dumont, escaped to the U.S.

The Metis and Cree resistance of 1885 was the final chapter of armed resistance in the 19th century. However, the use of military force in controlling Native peoples was already being bypassed by the Indian Act of 1876, itself a reaffirmation and expansion on previous legislation concerning Native peoples. This Act, with subsequent additions and changes, remains the basis of Native legislation in Canada today.

Under the Indian Act, the federal government through its Department of Indian Affairs is given complete control over the economic, social, and political affairs of Native communities. More than just a legislative instrument to administer "Indian affairs", the Indian Act was and is an attack on the very foundations of the First Nations as nations. Besides restricting hunting and fishing, criminalizing independent economic livelihood (i.e. in 1881 the Act made it illegal for Natives to "sell, barter or traffic fish"), the Act also declared who was and who was not an Indian, it removed "Indian status" from Native women who married non-Natives, and criminalized vital aspects of Native organization and culture such as the potlatch, the sun-dance, and pow-wow. Everything that formed the political, social, and economic bases of Native societies was restricted; the culture was attacked because it stood as the final barrier of resistance to European colonization. In the area of political organization,

> The Indian Act (of 1880) created a new branch of the civil service that was to be called the Department of Indian Affairs. It once again empowered the superintendent general to impose the elective system of band government... In addition, this new legisla-

> tion allowed the superintendent general to deprive the traditional leaders of recognition by stating that the only spokesmen of the band were those men elected according to...the Indian Act. [40]

In 1894, amendments to the Act authorized the forced relocation of Native children to residential boarding schools, which were seen as superior to schools on the reserves because they removed the children from the influence of the Native community. Isolated children in the total control of Europeans were easier to break; Native languages were forbidden and all customs, values, religious traditions and even clothing were to be replaced by European forms. Sexual and physical abuse were common characteristics of these schools, and their effects have been devastatingly effective in partially acculturating generations of Native peoples.

The Indian Act followed earlier legislation in that the long-term objective was the assimilation of Christianized Natives, gradually removing any "special status" for Native peoples and eliminating reserves and treaty rights; all of which would make the complete exploitation of the land a simple task. As part of this strategy of containing and repressing Native peoples who did not assimilate, and who were thus an obstacle to the full expansion of Canada, the Indian Act also denied the right to vote to Native peoples and implemented a pass system similar if not the forerunner to the Pass Laws in the Bantustans of South Africa (it should also be noted that Asian peoples were denied the right to vote as well and were subjected to viciously racist campaigns in BC by both the government and the labour movement; only in 1950 were Native and Asian peoples given this "illustrious" right).

---

40. John L. Tobias, op. cit., pg. 46.

1492   1820   1840

EXTERMINATION AND ASSIMILATION: TWO METHODS, ONE GOAL

In the early 1900s, the population of Native peoples in North America had reached their lowest point. In the U.S. alone this population had declined to some 250,000. As in Canada, Native peoples had been consigned to largely desolate land areas and the process of assimilation began through government agencies such as the Bureau of Indian Affairs. Here too, residential schools, criminalization of Native cultures, and control of political and economic systems were the instruments used. Native peoples, like those in Canada, were viewed as obstacles to be crushed in the drive for profits.

In both countries, resistance to this assimilation continued in various forms: potlatches and sun-dances were continued in clandestinity and the elected band councils opposed. As well, Native peoples began forming organizations to work against government polices. In 1912, the Alaska Native Brotherhood was formed by the Tlingit and Tsimshian at Sikta. That same year, the Nishga Land Claims Petition was presented to the Canadian government concerning the recognition of aboriginal title; no treaties had or have been signed with First Nations in BC [as of 1991]—with the exception of a north-eastern corner of BC included in Treaty No. 8 and some minor treaties on Vancouver Island. Yet Natives in BC had found themselves dispossessed of their territory and subjected to the Indian Act. In 1916 the Nishga joined with the interior Salish and formed another inter-tribal organization, the Allied Tribes of BC. Funds

Indigenous Land Within United States, 1492-1977

were raised, meetings held, and petitions sent to Ottawa. In 1927, a special Joint Committee of the Senate and House of Commons found that Natives had "not established any claim to the lands of BC based on aboriginal or other title." [41] That same year Section 141 was added to the Indian Act prohibiting raising money and prosecuting claims to land or retaining a lawyer.

While the European nations would lead the world into two great wars for hegemony, political instability and economic depredations formed the general pattern in South and Central America. Military regimes backed by U.S. and British imperialism carried out genocidal policies and severe repression against Indigenous peoples. As in North America, Indigenous peoples were consigned to desolate reserve lands where the state or missionaries retained control over political, economic, social and cultural systems. However, in contrast to the colonization of North America, where Native peoples were viewed as irrelevant to economic expansion, the Indians of South and Central America remained as substantial sources of exploited labour. With the large-scale investments from the imperialist centres in the form of loans, the export of primary resources took priority. The 'rubber boom' was one example, with tens of thousands of Indians dying in forced labour, relocations, and massacres carried out by major land owners, companies, and hired death squads.

> In the wake of the rubber boom, Colombia, Ecuador and Peru became battlegrounds for a war between oil companies. Subsidiaries of Shell and Exxon fought for exploration rights in the Amazon, even to the extent of becoming involved in a border war

41.   Quoted in Wilson Duff, op. cit., p. 69.

between Ecuador and Peru in 1941... In Brazil...87 Indian groups were wiped out in the first half of the 20th century from contact with expanding colonial frontiers—especially rubber and mining in the northwest, cattle in the northeast, agriculture in the south and east, and from road building throughout all regions. [42]

While policies of forced assimilation were occasionally articulated, military and paramilitary forces were to remain an essential part of controlling Native communities and opening up territories to exploitation. The most violent manifestation of this repression came in El Salvador in 1932, where as many as 30,000 people, primarily Indian peasants, were massacred following an uprising against the military dictatorship that took power the year prior. While the massacres were carried out under the guise of "anti-communism", U.S. and Canadian naval vessels stood offshore, and U.S. Marines in Nicaragua were put on alert. However, as the U.S. Chief of Naval Operations later testified before Congress, "it was found unnecessary for the U.S. ...and British forces to land, as the Salvadorian government had the situation in hand." [43] During the same period in Colombia, the Indian leader Quintin Lame helped initiate struggles for land and developed an Indigenous philosophy of resistance; in the early 1980s, his legacy would live on in the Indian guerrilla group "Commando Quintin Lame". Gonzalo Sanchez was another leader who helped organize the Supreme Council of Indians in Natagaima, Colombia, in 1920.

After World War II, significant changes in the world capitalist economy would see increased penetration of the Amazon and other lowland forest regions in South America. In the post-War period, the U.S. emerged in a dominant position in the world economy and would subsequently move to open up markets for economic expansion. In Western Europe and Japan, as part of the Marshall Plan, some $30 billion in loans and aid was pumped into the economies to rebuild these countries as U.S. markets and, not insignificantly, as a base of containment against the USSR (military alliances were also created through NATO and SEATO, positioned against the East Bloc).

---

42. Andrew Gray, op. cit., pg. 8.
43. Quoted in Noam Chomsky, *Turning the Tide: The U.S. and Latin America*, Black Rose Books, Montreal, 1987, pg. 44.

South and Central America were to be brought firmly under U.S. control, a process begun during the early 1900s as the U.S. moved to replace Britain as the dominant imperialist nation in the region, even paying off debts owed to Britain. As part of the U.S. post-War plans, South and Central America would also receive billions of dollars in direct financial aid from the U.S. and from private transnational banks. This aid al-

lowed the "underdeveloped" countries to industrialize by importing modern technology from the U.S. (in fact, as part of U.S. financial aid, the loans had to be spent in the U.S.). The enormous debts incurred in this process guaranteed dependence and opened up these countries to multinational corporations. As well, international organizations such as the World Bank, International Bank for Reconstruction and Development, and the Agency for International Development (AID) were formed to provide multilateral funding aimed largely at the agro-export sectors, resource extraction, hydro-electric projects and infrastructure (roads, communications, etc.) necessary for the development of those industries. Linked to this "aid" scheme is the International Monetary Fund, which doesn't fund specific projects but instead steps in with balance of payments support when a country is unable to pay its debts.

These projects and the overall industrialization opened up areas for further exploitation; penetration of areas such as the Amazon and large-scale expropriations accelerated in the 1960s, further devastating Indigenous peoples and leading to renewed campaigns of extermination.

Of course, all this economic restructuring did not occur without growing resistance. With growing movements against imperialism, including peasant unions, students, workers, guerrillas and Indians, a substantial part of the "aid" included military training, weapons, and equipment. U.S. Special Forces troopers were not only in Southeast Asia, they were also quite busy in Central America, training death squads and directing massacres. As part of an overall counterinsurgency campaign, the militarization precipitated an upward spiral of violence. In Guatemala alone, between 1966–68, some 8,000 people were slaughtered by Guatemalan soldiers under the direction of U.S. Green Beret advisors; U.S. pilots flew U.S. planes on bombing missions. Paramilitary groups/death squads hunted down "subversives" in collaboration with the government, military, multinationals, and land-owners.[44] The main targets of this campaign, dubbed "Operation Guatemala", were the Mayan peoples.

Another aspect of the counter-insurgency plans was that of population control. Primarily the focus of U.S. state-funding, the Agency for International Development (AID) was established in 1961. Using the false pretext of "over-population problem", instead of imperialism, as the cause of mass poverty and starvation, population control came to be championed as the most important dilemma facing the "modern world". Under the guise of "family planning", AID began funding for a wide-range of public and private organizations, foundations, and churches who provided training, equipment, and clinics for birth control programs. Between 1968 and 1972, "funds earmarked for population programs through legislation and obligated by AID amounted to more than $250 million".[45] South America received the largest percentage of this funding. Besides educational material, birth control pills, IUDs, and other pharmaceuticals developed by a profitable gene and biotechnology industry in the imperialist centres, the main thrust of population control remains sterilization. Between 1965–71, an estimated 1 million women in Brazil had been sterilized.[46] In Puerto Rico, 34% of all women of child-bearing age had been sterilized by 1965.[47] Between 1963–65, more than 40,000 women in Colombia had been sterilized.[48] In contrast to these programs in the "Third World", the imperialist centres see restrictions on abortion and struggles for women's reproductive choice. But even here there is a double standard for non-European women:

44. Tom Barry, Deb Preusch, and Beth Wood, *Dollars and Dictators*, Grove Press Inc., New York, 1983, pg. 122.

45. Bonnie Mass, *The Political Economy of Population Control in Latin America*, Editions Latin America, Montreal, 1972, pg. 8.

46. Ibid, pg. 19.

47. Ibid, pg. 41.

48. "Growing Fight Against Sterilization of Native Women", *Akwesasne Notes* Vol. 11 No. 1, Winter 1979, pg. 29.

Lee Brightman, United Native Americans President, estimates that of the Native population of 800,000 (in the U.S.), as many as 42% of the women of childbearing age and 10% of the men...have been sterilized... The first official inquiry into the sterilization of Native women...by Dr. Connie Uri...reported that 25,000 Indian women had been permanently sterilized within Indian Health Services facilities alone through 1975... According to a 1970 fertilization study, 20% of married Black women had been sterilized, almost three times the percentage of white married women. There was a 180% rise in the number of sterilizations performed during 1972–73 in New York City municipal hospitals which serve predominantly Puerto Rican neighbourhoods. [49]

Similar results were found in Inuit communities in the Northwest Territories. Clearly, "overpopulation" is not an issue in North America, nor is it in South or Central America. Rather, it is a method for reducing specific portions of the population who would organize against their oppression and who have no place in the schemes of capital. In other words, "It is more effective to kill guerrillas in the womb".

Of all the South American countries that underwent massive industrialization after World War II, Brazil is probably the most well known. Following a 1964 coup backed by the U.S., IMF and multinationals, foreign investment rose steadily. Between 1964–71, over $4 billion had been pumped into Brazil through the World Bank, AID, IDB, and others. [50]

Between 1900–57, the Indigenous population of Brazil had declined from over 1 million to less than 200,000[51] through the rubber boom, ranching, and mining industries. Following the 1964 coup and the rise in foreign investment, the penetration of the Amazon region in particular was increased. As these industries invaded even more Indian lands, a renewed campaign of extermination accompanied them. Indians were hunted down by death squads, their communities bombed and massacred, and disease epidemics purposely spread through injections and infected blankets. In the 1960s alone,

Of the 19,000 Monducurus believed to have existed in the 30s, only 1200 were left. The strength of the Guaranis had been reduced from 5,000 to 300. There were 400 Carajas left out of

49. Ibid, pg. 29.
50. *Supysaua: A Documentary Report on the Conditions of Indian Peoples in Brazil*, Indigena Inc. and American Friends of Brazil, Nov. 1974, pg. 48.
51. Ibid, pg. 6.
52. Norman Lewis, "Genocide", *Supysaua* op. cit., pg. 9.

4,000. Of the Cintas Largas, who had been attacked from the air and driven into the mountains, possibly 500 had survived out of 10,000... Some like the Tapaiunas—in this case from a gift of sugar laced with arsenic—had disappeared altogether.[52]

All these atrocities were part of a "pacification" campaign aimed at eliminating the Indians, who here too were seen as obstacles to "development". The government agencies responsible for "Indian affairs" were some of the worst agents in this campaign, so much so that the poorly-named Indian Protection Service had to be disbanded and replaced by the National Indian Foundation (FUNAI). Not surprisingly, the only real changes were in the names. By 1970, plans for building an extensive road system for all the industries that had recently invaded the Amazon were announced. The following year, the president of FUNAI signed a decree which read "Assistance to the Indian will be as complete as possible, but cannot obstruct national development nor block the various axes of penetration into the Amazon region."[53] The Trans-Amazonic road system resulted in the forced relocation of some 25 Indian nations and thousands of deaths. The struggle against the roads continues today.

Brazil is only one example; similar developments occurred in other South American countries.

Seemingly in contrast to these extermination campaigns, Canada appeared to be moving towards a much more "liberal" epoch; why, Natives had even been given the "right" to vote, the pass laws had been scrapped, and potlatches were once again permitted! In fact, the Indian Act itself was being viewed by some as an impediment to the assimilation of Native peoples. The combined effects of the Indian Act, the residential schools, etc. had so debilitated Native peoples that they were almost no longer needed; once powerful cultural bases, such as the potlatch, were reduced to near spectacles for the enjoyment of Euro-Canadians similar to rodeo shows. By 1969, the government went so far as to articulate its goals in the aptly-named "White Paper"; the intent was to end the special legal and constitutional status of Natives, and to deny the relevancy of treaty rights. Ostensibly a policy to "help" the Indian, the paper even suggested a total revision of the Indian Act and a gradual phasing out of the Department of Indian Affairs over a five year period. In the denial of treaty rights and land claims, the paper stated,

---

53.   "The Politics of Genocide Against the Indians of Brazil", *Supysaua* op. cit., pg. 35.
54.   Government of Canada, *Statement of the Government of Canada on Indian Policy*, 1969, pg. 11.

> These aboriginal claims to land are so general and undefined that it is not realistic to think of them as specific claims capable of remedy except through a policy and program that will end injustice to Indians as members of the Canadian community. [54]

During the same period, Canada was moving towards increased resource extraction. This had begun in the 1950s especially in the mining of uranium for nuclear energy and as export for the U.S. nuclear energy and weapons industry. Uranium mining was centred primarily in Saskatchewan and in the U.S. southwest. As well, there was increased oil and gas exploration in the North and the development of hydroelectric projects. What better way to push through these dangerous and damaging projects than by accelerating the government's long-term assimilation policy and denying Native land title? Clearly, extermination campaigns in Brazil and assimilation policies in Canada are two sides of the same coin: destroying Native nations and opening up the lands to further exploration. What these governments didn't count on was the continued resistance of Native people.

THE PEOPLE AIM FOR FREEDOM

Along with an explosion of international struggles in the 1960s, including national liberation movements in Afrika, Asia, and in the Americas, there was an upsurge in Native people's resistance. This upsurge found its background in the continued struggles of Native peoples and the development of the struggle against continued resource extraction throughout the Americas.

In South and Central America Native resistance grew alongside the student, worker, women's and guerrilla movements, which were comprised largely of Mestizos in the urban centres.

In Ecuador, the Shuar nation had formed a federation based on regional associations of Shuar communities in 1964, and was influential in the development of other Indigenous organizations; it would also be the focus of government repression as in 1969 when its main offices were burnt down and its leaders attacked and imprisoned. In 1971, the Indigenous Regional Council of Cauca (CRIC) was formed in Colombia by 2,000 Indians from 10 communities. CRIC quickly initiated a campaign for recuperating stolen reserve lands. In Bolivia, two Aymaran organizations were formed: the Mink'a and the Movimiento Tupac Katari. National and international conferences were held in various countries, and by 1974 a conference in Paraguay drew delegates from every country in South and Central America from a large number of Indian nations.

A primary focus of these Indigenous movements was recuperating stolen lands, and widespread occupations, protests, and road blockades were organized. In Chile, Mapuches began "fence-running"—moving fences which separated reserve lands from farm lands and extending the reserve territory. In Mexico, Indigenous peasants carried out large-scale occupations: by 1975 there were 76 occupations in Sinaloa alone, and some 25,000 acres of land occupied in Sinaloa and Sonora. By December of 1976, tens of thousands occupied land in Sonora, Sinaloa, Durango, and Coahuila.[55] Of course, these and many other occupations and protests did not occur without severe repression. Assassinations, massacres, destruction of communities, and scorched earth policies were directed against the Indigenous movements.

---

55. Jane Adams, "Mexico—The Struggle for the Land", *Indigena* Vol. 3 No. 1, Summer 1977, pg. 28, 30.

Similarly, the reclaiming of traditional Indian lands was also a primary focus of struggle in North America. One of the first of these occupations in this period was the seizing of the Seaway International Bridge in Ontario by Mohawks, in December 1968. The action was to protest the Canadian state's decision to levy customs duties on goods carried across the international border by Mohawks, despite a treaty which

stipulated this right and the fact that the border area was on Mohawk land. The occupation ended when RCMP and Ontario Provincial Police stormed the bridge and arrested 48 Mohawks. However, the struggle of the Mohawks was to precipitate occupations which were to follow as a "Red Nationalism / Red Power" movement swept across both Canada and the U.S., alongside Black, Chicano, and Puerto Rican liberation movements.

In 1968, the American Indian Movement (AIM) was formed in Minneapolis-St. Paul. At first an organization modeled after Euro-American Left groups and inspired in part by the Civil Rights struggles of the 1950s and 60s, as well as the Black Panthers, AIM organized against police violence, racism, and poverty. Initially urban-based and predominantly centred in the Dakotas and Nebraska, AIM quickly became a widespread movement represented in both urban ghettos and rural reserve areas.

Although AIM members would be involved in many of the struggles that would develop—partly because AIM was an international movement and not regional—AIM itself was only one part of the "Red Nationalist" movement. In 1968, the National Alliance for Red Power had formed on the West Coast, and the following year Indians occupied Alcatraz Island in San Francisco harbour, claiming they had "discovered" it; the occupation would last 19 months and would become known as the first major event in the struggle for "Red Power". Another aspect of this period was the continuing local and regional daily struggles, independent though not totally unrelated from the emerging Native liberation movement, in communities fighting theft of land, poverty, pollution, etc. In 1970, for example, 200 Metis and Indians occupied the Alberta New Start Centre at Lac La Biche, protesting against the federal government's cancellation of the program.

That same year, AIM participated in the occupation of Plymouth Rock and the Mayflower ship replica on "Thanksgiving Day", as well as organizing protests and actions against the BIA (Bureau of Indian Affairs). In South Dakota, a protest at the Custer Courthouse was attacked by police, leading to a riot in which the court and several buildings were burned down. In 1972, AIM organized the "Trail of Broken Treaties Caravan", and prepared a 20 point position paper concerning the general conditions of Native peoples in the U.S. The Trail ended in Washington, DC, where demonstrators occupied and destroyed the offices of the BIA.

The following year, traditionalists in the Pine Ridge reservation in South Dakota requested AIM support after a campaign of terror led by Tribal President Dick Wilson and BIA thugs. On February 27, a caravan of people went to Wounded Knee for a council—the site of the 1890 massacre. The area was almost immediately surrounded by police, and a one day meeting turned into a 71 day armed occupation in which 300 people resisted a large military and paramilitary force consisting of FBI agents, BIA police, local and state police, and military personnel. Two Natives were shot dead, two wounded, and one Federal Agent wounded. Three weeks into the liberation of Wounded Knee, the Independent Oglala Nation was established.

> The Independent Oglala Nation was more than just a brave gesture by a band of besieged Indians. It represented the gravest threat in more than a century to the plans of the U.S. government to subdue the Native people of the U.S. and to deprive them of their lands for the exploitation and profit of white interests.[56]

As supplies dwindled and the military prepared for a final assault, the defenders decided to withdraw. On May 7, about half the people filtered through the enemy lines, and the following day about 150 who remained laid down their arms. In the period following, the FBI, BIA, and Wilson's regime conducted a campaign of terror; by 1976 as many as 250 people in and around Pine Ridge were dead, including 50 members of AIM. Shootings, firebombings, assaults, and assassinations were carried out by Wilson's goons and in conjunction with the FBI's Counter-Intelligence Program (COINTELPRO). On June 26, 1975, an FBI raid on an AIM en-

---

56. "On the Road to Wounded Knee", *Indian Nation* Vol. 3, No. 1, April 1976, pg. 15.

campment resulted in a fire-fight in which two FBI agents and an Oglala, Joseph Stuntz, were shot dead. Although Stuntz' death was never investigated, nor were the many other killings of Oglala traditionalists and AIM members during this period, the FBI launched a campaign to imprison AIM members for the two dead agents. Eventually Leonard Peltier would be convicted of the killings in a trial that showed nothing more than that the FBI had fabricated evidence and testimony.

In the same year as the liberation of Wounded Knee, AIM was also established in Canada following the Cache Creek highway blockade in BC. The blockade was against poor housing conditions on a nearby Native reserve. In November of that year, the Indian Affairs office in Kenora, Ontario was occupied for one day by Ojibways. The following year, members of the Ojibway Warrior's Society and AIM initiated an armed occupation of Anicinabe Park, near Kenora, from July 22 to August 8. Two months earlier, Mohawks from Akwesasne and Kahnawake had occupied Moss Lake in upper state New York, reclaiming and renaming the area Ganienkeh—Land of the Flint, the traditional name for the Kanienkehake, People of the Flint. After a shooting incident between White vigilantes and Mohawks, police insisted on entering Ganienkeh to investigate but were refused entry. As the threat of a police raid increased, Natives, including some veterans from Wounded Knee, rushed to Ganienkeh. Bunkers were built and defensive lines established. In the end, police withdrew (in 1977, the Mohawks agreed to leave Moss Lake in exchange for land in Clinton County, which is closer to Kahnawake and Akwesasne).

On September 14, 1974, the "Native People's Caravan" left Vancouver, initiated by Natives who had participated in the Anicinabe Park occupation. Similar to the Trail of Broken Treaties, the Caravan demanded recognition and respect for treaty and aboriginal rights, settlement of Native land claims, an end to the Indian Act, and an investigation of the

Department of Indian Affairs by Natives aimed at dissolving it. By September 30th, the Caravan had brought around 800–900 Natives to Parliament Hill in Ottawa. Instead of a meeting with parliament, the protest faced riot police and barricades. As police attacked the demonstration, clashes broke out, leaving dozens of Natives and nine police injured.

In 1976, the "Trail of Self-Determination" left the west coast of the U.S. as one of many anti-Bicentennial protests organized by Native peoples. Its purpose was to get the government's answer to the points raised by the 1972 caravan. As in that protest, government officials refused to meet with the people and 47 demonstrators were arrested at the BIA offices in Washington, DC.

It was also during this period that Native peoples began organizing around international bodies. In the U.S., members of AIM and numerous traditional leaders and elders formed the International Indian Treaty Conference, in 1974.

> The thrust of the Treaty Conference is for recognition of treaties by the U.S. as a means of restoring sovereign relations between the native nations and that country. Then, there will be moves to control exploitation, return control of native lands to...the native nation, and a return of forms of government appropriate to each nation. [57]

The IITC was the first Indian organization to apply for and receive UN Non-Governmental status. Delegates from the IITC, CRIC, and other South and Central American Indigenous organizations formed the basis for developing legalistic frameworks based on international laws aimed at restoring sovereign nation status for First Nations. Conferences such as the 1977 UN-sponsored NGO meeting on "problems of Western Hemisphere Indigenous Peoples" or the Fourth International Russell Tribunal in 1980, were organized to examine and document the continuation of genocidal practises, and to develop policies concerning these issues. The end result of these conferences appears to be a forum for documenting genocide, and, at best, exerting some level of international pressure on particular countries. As AIM member Russell Means has stated, "It appears useless to appeal to the U.S. or its legal system to restore its honor by honoring its treaties." [58] In light of the recent UN role in the U.S.-led Gulf War, and its recent repeal of the condemnation of Zionism as racism, the UN itself seems useless.

---

57. "North American Sovereign Nations", *Akwesasne Notes* Vol. 8 No. 4, pg. 16.
58. *Akwesasne Notes* Vol. 8 No. 6.

THE STRUGGLE FOR LAND

As previously discussed, the world economic system underwent profound changes following and as a result of the Second World War. In the post-War economic boom, plans for new energy policies began to be formulated in the U.S. and Canada. As already noted, one aspect of these plans was based on uranium mining and its application in nuclear energy and weapons systems. As well, plans for diverting water and/or hydro-electric power from Canada to the U.S. were also formulated in 1964 through the North

Cree child opposed to James Bay 2 hydro development in Northern Quebec

American Water and Power Alliance (NAWAPA). Following the 1973 "Oil Crisis", plans for developing "internal" energy sources were intensified. In the U.S., this energy policy was dubbed "Project Independence".

> It seems clear that the U.S. government has anticipated that American natives—like those of other colonized areas of the world who have tried to resist the theft of their natural resources—might put up a fight... [T]his seems the most logical conclusion to draw from Senate Bill 826, an expansion of the Federal Energy Act of 1974 into a U.S. centred 'comprehensive energy policy'. Section 616 of this Bill proposes that the Energy Administrator 'is authorized to provide for participation of military personnel in the performance of his functions' and that armed forces personnel so assigned will be, in effect, an independent 'energy army', under the direct control of the Department of Energy. [59]

59. Paula Giese, "The Last Indian War: For Energy" *Report on the Third International Indian Treaty Conference*, June 15–19, 1977.

As well, in 1971 a group of electrical power generation companies and government resources bureaucrats issued the North Central Power Study, "which proposed the development of coal strip mining in Montana, Wyoming, and the Dakotas..." [60]

In Canada, these plans can be seen in the hydro-electric projects built in Manitoba and in James Bay, northern Quebec. There was also the penetration of the Canadian north with oil and gas exploration, the Mackenzie Valley pipeline, uranium mining in Saskatchewan, etc. In the U.S., the new energy policies precipitated various attacks on Native nations.

In 1974, Public Law 93-531 was passed authorizing the partition of joint Hopi and Navajo lands in northern Arizona and the forced relocation of some 13,000 people. The purpose of the relocation was ostensibly to resolve a false "Hopi-Navajo land dispute". In fact, there are some 19 billion tons of coal in this land. Another example is that of Wounded Knee. During World War II, a northwestern portion of the Pine Ridge reservation was "borrowed" by the federal government for use as an aerial gunnery range. It was to be returned when the war ended.

> Well, the war ended in 1945 and along about 1970, some of the traditional people on the reserve started asking 'Where is our land? We want it back'. What had happened was that a certain agency...NASA, had circled a satellite and that satellite was circled in co-operation with...the National Uranium Research and Evaluations Institute... What they discovered was that there was a particularly rich uranium deposit within...the gunnery range. [61]

Dick Wilson was put in place as Tribal Council President, financed, supplied and backed by the government, with the purpose of having him sign over the gunnery range lands to the U.S. government. On June 26, 1975, Dick Wilson signed this 10 per cent of the Pine Ridge reserve land to the federal government on the same day that the FBI raided the AIM encampment.

> In a period barely exceeding 200 years, the 100% of the territory which was in Indigenous hands in 1600, was reduced to 10% and over the next 100 years to 3%. We retain nominal rights

---

60. Ibid.
61. Ward Churchill, "Leonard Peltier, Political Prisoner: A Case History of the Land Rip-Offs", *Red Road* #2, June 1991, pg. 6.

to about 3% of our original territory within the USA today. Native peoples were consigned to what was thought to be the most useless possible land... Ironically, from the perspective of the Predator, this turned out to be the land which contained about 2/3 of what the U.S. considers to be its domestic uranium reserve. Perhaps 25% of the readily accessible low-sulphur coal. Perhaps 1/5 of the oil and natural gas. Virtually all of the copper and bauxite... There is gold. There are renewable resources and water rights in the arid west. [62]

Similar comparisons can be found in Canada and the countries of South and Central America. With massive changes in industrialization and in energy demands, along with new technologies in locating and extracting resources, the colonization process has, since the Second World War, entered a new phase. Along with these flashpoints arising from the "Last Indian War: For Energy", there are the daily demands of capital in other industries such as forestry, fishing, rubber, agriculture, ranching, etc. and in land for military weapons testing, training, etc.

Taking into account these developments since World War II, and the colonization process prior to it, an understanding of the history of Indigenous resistance becomes more clear. Most importantly, however, this resistance continues today.

---

62.   Ibid, pg. 6.

IN TOTAL RESISTANCE

"Now that war is being forced upon us, we will turn our hearts and minds to war and it too we will wage with all our might... Our Spirits are strong. We are together at last with ourselves and the world of our ancestors; we are proud before our children and our generations unborn... We are free. No yoke of white government oppression can contain us. We are free."

–Mohawk Nation Office, *August 27, 1990*

In March 1990, the Mohawks of Kanesatake occupied the Pines—traditional lands which also contain the peoples cemetery and a lacrosse field—against the Municipality of Oka's plans to expand an adjacent golf course over the Pines. The golf course expansion was part of Oka's plans to expand a lucrative tourist industry. On July 11, over 100 members of the Quebec Provincial Police (SQ) attacked the barricades, opening fire on mostly women and children and firing tear-gas and concussion grenades. Members of the Kahnawake Warrior's Society and warriors from Kanesatake returned fire. In the exchange of fire, one SQ officer was killed. Following the fire-fight in the Pines and the retreat of the police, Warriors from Kahnawake seized the Mercier Bridge—a major commuter bridge into Montreal—to deter a second SQ attack. More barricades were erected on roads and highways around both Kanesatake and Kahnawake by hundreds of Mohawk women and men—setting into motion one of the longest armed stand-offs in North America in recent history. The stand-off, which saw hundreds of police and over 4,000 troops from the Canadian Armed Forces deployed, initiated widespread solidarity from Native peoples across Canada; road and railway blockades were erected, Indian Affairs offices occupied, demonstrations held, and sabotage carried out against railway bridges and electrical power lines. The vulnerability of such infrastructure was well known, and in fact this possibility of an escalation of Native resistance was a main part of why there was no massacre carried out against the Natives and supporters who held out in the Treatment Centre. On September 26, the last remaining defenders made the collective decision to disengage—not surrender—and began to move out of the area. They were, in theory, walking home, refusing to surrender for they had committed no "crimes" in defending sovereign Mohawk land. Needless to say, the colonialist occupation forces disagreed and captured the defenders, subjecting some of the Warriors to torture including beatings and mock executions.

At the same time, members of the Peigan Lonefighter's Society had diverted the sacred Oldman River away from a dam system in Alberta and confronted the RCMP. Milton Born With A Tooth would subsequently be arrested for firing two warning shots into the air. He has since been sentenced to 18 months.

As well, the Lil'wat nation in BC erected road blockades on their traditional land in an assertion of their sovereignty and as part of the solidarity campaign with the Mohawks. Four months later the RCMP would raid the blockade and arrest some 50 Lil'wat and supporters, on November 6. On November 24, a logging operation on Lubicon Cree land in northern Alberta was attacked and some $20,000 damage inflicted on vehicles and equipment. Thirteen Lubicon Cree including Chief Bernard Ominayak were subsequently charged with the action but have yet to be put on trial. They have refused to recognize the trial as having any jurisdiction on Lubicon Cree land.

During the same period, Indigenous peoples in South America were carrying forward their struggles.

In Bolivia in October 1990, some 800 Indians from the Amazon region—Moxenos, Yuracares, Chimanes and Guaranies—walked 330 miles from the northern city of Trinidad to La Paz in a month-long "March for Land and Dignity". When the march reached the mountain pass that separates the highlands from the Amazon plains, thousands of Aymaras, Quechuas and Urus from across the Bolivian highlands were there to greet them. Like the struggles of their sisters and brothers in North America, this march was against logging operations as well as cattle ranching on Indian land.

In Ecuador, from June 4th to 8th, 1990, a widespread Indigenous uprising paralyzed the country. Nearly all major roads and highways were blocked, demonstrations and festivals of up to 50,000 spread throughout the country, despite massive police and military repression. Demonstrations were attacked, protesters beaten, tear-gassed and shot. Through the coordination of CONAIE (Confederacion de Nacionalidades del Ecuador)—a national Indian organization formed in 1986—a 16 point "Mandate for the Defense, Life, and Rights of the Indigenous Nationalities" was released. The demands included control of Indian lands, constitutional and tax reforms, and the dissolution of various government-controlled pseudo-Indian organizations. The government agreed to negotiations on the demands; the uprising had restricted food supplies to the urban areas, disrupted water and electricity supply, closed down schools, and occupied oil wells, airports, and radio stations. The Indigenous uprising had effectively shut down the country.

In this way, the Campaign for 500 Years of Indigenous Resistance in 1992 forms an important point in this history: "In our continent, history can be divided into 3 phases; before the arrival of the invaders; these five hundred years; and that period, beginning today, which we must define and build" (Campaign 500 Years of Resistance and Popular Resistance).

IN THE SPIRIT OF CRAZY HORSE
IN THE SPIRIT OF TUPAC KATARI
IN TOTAL RESISTANCE

ABOUT PM PRESS

PM Press was founded at the end of 2007 by a small collection of folks with decades of publishing, media, and organizing experience. PM co-founder Ramsey Kanaan started AK Press as a young teenager in Scotland almost 30 years ago and, together with his fellow PM Press co-conspirators, has published and distributed hundreds of books, pamphlets, CDs, and DVDs. Members of PM have founded enduring book fairs, spearheaded victorious tenant organizing campaigns, and worked closely with bookstores, academic conferences, and even rock bands to deliver political and challenging ideas to all walks of life. We're old enough to know what we're doing and young enough to know what's at stake.

We seek to create radical and stimulating fiction and non-fiction books, pamphlets, t-shirts, visual and audio materials to entertain, educate and inspire you. We aim to distribute these through every available channel with every available technology - whether that means you are seeing anarchist classics at our bookfair stalls; reading our latest vegan cookbook at the café; downloading geeky fiction e-books; or digging new music and timely videos from our website.

PM Press is always on the lookout for talented and skilled volunteers, artists, activists and writers to work with. If you have a great idea for a project or can contribute in some way, please get in touch.

PM Press
PO Box 23912
Oakland, CA 94623
www.pmpress.org

FRIENDS OF PM PRESS

These are indisputably momentous times – the financial system is melting down globally and the Empire is stumbling. Now more than ever there is a vital need for radical ideas.

In the year since its founding – and on a mere shoestring – PM Press has risen to the formidable challenge of publishing and distributing knowledge and entertainment for the struggles ahead. We have published an impressive and stimulating array of literature, art, music, politics, and culture. Using every available medium, we've succeeded in connecting those hungry for ideas and information to those putting them into practice.

Friends of PM allows you to directly help impact, amplify, and revitalize the discourse and actions of radical writers, filmmakers, and artists. It provides us with a stable foundation from which we can build upon our early successes and provides a much-needed subsidy for the materials that can't necessarily pay their own way.

It's a bargain for you too. For a minimum of $25 a month, you'll get all the audio and video (over a dozen CDs and DVDs in our first year) or all of the print releases (also over a dozen in our first year). For $40 you'll get everything that is published in hard copy. Friends also have the ability to purchase any/all items from our webstore at a 50% discount. And what could be better than the thrill of receiving a monthly package of cutting edge political theory, art, literature, ideas and practice delivered to your door?

Your card will be billed once a month, until you tell us to stop. Or until our efforts succeed in bringing the revolution around. Or the financial meltdown of Capital makes plastic redundant. Whichever comes first.

For more information on the Friends of PM, and about sponsoring particular projects, please go to www.pmpress.org, or contact us at: info@pmpress.org.